TABLOID SECRETS

TABLOID SECRETS

THE STORIES BEHIND THE HEADLINES AT THE WORLD'S MOST FAMOUS NEWSPAPER

NEVILLE THURLBECK

Biteback Publishing

First published in Great Britain in 2015 by
Biteback Publishing Ltd
Westminster Tower
3 Albert Embankment
London SE1 7SP
Copyright © Neville Thurlbeck 2015

ISBN 978-1-84954-853-3

10 9 8 7 6 5 4 3 2 1

A CIP catalogue record for this book is available from the British Library.

Set in Minion Pro

Printed and bound in Great Britain by
CPI Group (UK) Ltd, Croydon CR0 4YY

MIX
Paper from
responsible sources
FSC
www.fsc.org   FSC® C020471

To my wife, Boo and Bee, my family and special chums, and Ralphie, my Border terrier. For your love and laughter.

CONTENTS

PROLOGUE

IN PENNING THIS little memoir, I have tried to give a flavour of what life was like working for Fleet Street tabloids during the 1980s, '90s and up to the closure of the *News of the World* in 2011.

Since then, there has a been whole sea change in the way the tabloids report their news and the types of stories they cover. The Leveson Inquiry, numerous police investigations and a torrent of criticism (to put it mildly) from outraged celebrities and politicians have seen to that, for better or for worse.

But for a quarter of a century, I helped the red-top newspapers dole out their daily fare of scandals and exposés with cavalier abandon. And the British public bought into it in their millions.

It is a world that has vanished for good. And it is an insight into this very bizarre career which I thought you might be interested in seeing, through the eyes of a man who spent his life there. I hope you find it an entertaining read.

If none of you read it, it will at least provide future generations of my family with a lasting monument to the absurd and bonkers world of their bizarre ancestor!

Those of you looking for an insight into the phone-hacking saga will be disappointed. I think most of you will now be fed up to the back teeth with the wall-to-wall coverage of it over the past several years. And I don't want this book to be boring, self-serving guff. And I have no wish to heap piles of blame on anyone, many of whom are suffering greatly as I write. Finally, to focus on phone-hacking would distort the narrative, as it came onto my radar less than a handful of times in twenty-five years. That it came onto my radar at all is, of course, extremely regrettable and I apologise to anyone affected by it.

You will also hear very little of my wife and children, as I don't want them to become part of this story, although they are a large part of my 'normal' life.

While I covered hundreds of stories for the *News of the World*, the *Today* newspaper and the *Daily Mirror*, I have picked out a dozen or so which I hope give a flavour of how we worked in those ruthless, cut-throat times.

For a young man, they were an adventure. One minute, you could find yourself in the middle of an Alfred Hitchcock thriller. Next, a Marx Brothers comedy. Another, a Jacobean tragedy. It was never dull and I hope this book is a fair reflection of the industry I now look back on with fondness and astonishment.

CHAPTER 1

THE EARLY YEARS

THE EXPRESSION 'GENTEEL** poverty' could have been invented to describe my family. I was born in the front bedroom of 33 Merle Terrace, Sunderland, in what was then Co. Durham, on 7 October 1961.

It was just after breakfast, so as the midwife held me up to slap my bottom, my first view from the Victorian sash window would have been of thousands of men marching to work in the shipyards. Their tightly belted raincoats, flat caps and old gas mask haversacks slung over their shoulders carrying their lunchtime 'bait' was a daily sight in that town, which prided itself on its heavy industrial heritage. Some of the older men still wore hobnailed boots, striking the occasional spark which played on the cobbles at dusk.

We lived on the main road, which was just a five-minute walk downhill to the world-famous Doxford shipyard. Together with Laing's, Thompson's, Clarke's, Short's, Austin's, Bartram's and the Corporation Yard, they produced a quarter of the nation's shipping during the Second World War, an

1

impressive 1.5 million tons. Sunderland was by then the biggest shipbuilding town in the world, and ships and engineering were fixed in my family's DNA.

My maternal grandfather, Jack Tunstall, worked at Doxford's as an engineer. On my father's side, the Thurl family had arrived as Viking invaders and established a settlement near the source of the river Wear. *Bekkr* is Old Norse for stream or brook and the name gradually morphed into Thurlbeck. And there we remained for the best part of a millennium.

For most of the nineteenth century and into the early twentieth, the Thurlbecks were river pilots. Their task was to board large ships coming into port and carefully navigate them around the dangerous sandbanks at the mouth of the river Wear, and the jobs were passed from fathers to sons.

The landscape and lifestyle into which I was born will seem to some like another world but was the norm in post-war northern England. We had an outside lavatory, no telephone and no car. And we never went 'abroad'. In my family, anywhere outside England was simply classed as 'abroad'. It was dismissed as a place of no consequence – 'Why would we want to go *abroad* for?' So our holidays were taken in Devon, the Lake District or at my aunt and uncle's home in the Buckinghamshire countryside. And for something a little more exotic, Wales or Scotland, with my mother cheering, 'Look, we're crossing the border now!' as we all clapped and wondered at the sheer vastness of our journey in our 1960 Ford Classic.

The holidays at my aunt Margaret and uncle Warren's in

the 1960s and early '70s were idyllic and provide me today with my happiest childhood memories. I am still incredibly close to them. At their little cottage in a peaceful, pretty little village, I had my first glimpse of another type of England, completely different to the one I'd been brought up in. Fields of barley sprouted from pleasingly rounded and evenly eroded hillocks of chalk. The average Buckinghamshire man and woman still spoke with a distinctive, slightly West Country burr, now long since vanished. And the elongated summers seemed to turn everyone an attractive light tan, rather than the sallow hue of the average Wearsider, who lived beneath slate-grey skies.

My uncle Warren was and still is full of mischievous, schoolboy charm; my aunt Margaret – my mother's cousin – one of the most enchanting and elegant ladies I've ever met. To be with them was huge fun. And, together with my parents, I saw the picture-postcard Bucks countryside with its church-steepled villages. There were trips along the Thames on riverboats, Disraeli's house at Hughenden, biplanes at Old Warden aerodrome and a fabulous toy shop in Old Beaconsfield, where I once saw the actress Dame Margaret Rutherford in 1969, giving me my first glimpse of a celebrity.

There would be day trips to London, too. There were two highly exotic areas of London that really captured my imagination. Shaftesbury Avenue with its theatres cheek by jowl and the names of the great and the good up in lights – Ralph Richardson and John Gielgud in *No Man's Land*, Donald

Sinden and Frank Thornton in *Shut Your Eyes and Think of England* and John Quayle and Penelope Keith in *Donkeys' Years*. This was my first taste of proper theatre. I'd scour the listings pages of the *Sunday Times* to see if I could spot anyone famous appearing in the West End and off we'd all go, via the Tube from Amersham, to the Globe or Wyndham's. From the age of around ten, I was mesmerised by the magical world beyond the proscenium arch, and the passion has never left me.

The second area of intrigue to me was Fleet Street. In 1968, it was the epicentre of the biggest and best newspaper operation in the world. I recall being taken aback that the newspaper offices were all so close together, and have a vivid memory of my uncle taking us there, simply to look at the buildings. During one of our London visits, he paid the taxi driver five shillings as we stepped out in front of the *Daily Express*'s art deco office just a few seconds' walk from the *Daily Telegraph*, resplendent with its masthead, which conveyed gravitas and importance. Around the corner, in Bouverie Street, the jaunty, almost Wild West-style lettering of the *News of the World* masthead lay at the other end of the spectrum.

It would be inaccurate to say I felt that my future lay here. But I do remember being deeply impressed with this little village's power to communicate. It seemed incredible to my young mind that in this street, men and women clattered away on typewriters. And by some miracle, the following day this somehow materialised into a newspaper put through a letterbox in Sunderland. I had the sense that Fleet Street really mattered. That it did something utterly fascinating and worthwhile. But that it was all very unfair for it to be based entirely in this street, 300 miles away. A hopeless aspiration. But a lasting impression had been made.

As well as creating a lifetime of love and affection for my aunt and uncle, these holidays opened my young eyes to possibilities further afield than Sunderland. From the age of ten, I knew that when I left home, it would be for 'the south'.

Apart from my grandfather Tunstall's brothers John and William, who were killed on the Western Front in 1915 and 1917 aged seventeen and nineteen, and my mother Audrey's weekend coach trip to Paris with a girlfriend in 1955, I was the first member of the family in living memory to set foot on foreign soil, in 1981, when I was nineteen.

After setting up their Viking camp on the Wear, the Thurlbecks had remained resolutely intimidated by the notion of travel ever since. In fact, my father's father, the identically named Thomas Edward, often repeated a story of how, as a young man in the 1920s depression, he was forced to take a job as a train guard. After falling asleep in the guard's van on a train from Sunderland to Middlesbrough, where he was due to get off, he eventually woke up at Doncaster.

I only have two memories of my grandfather Thurlbeck. My first was Christmas and he'd bought me a small train set. As we played with it on the floor of his home, he pointed to the guard's van and said he used to sit in one like it as a young man. He added: 'I went to Doncaster once, you know.' Even at five years old, I remember being distinctly underwhelmed by this achievement. My second and last memory of this quiet, modest, moderate man was being taken to see him as he lay on his deathbed a few months later as lung cancer ravaged his once athletic frame. In his youth, he had been a brilliant footballer who was awarded a contract with Charlton Athletic in the 1920s, only for my grandmother to ban him from moving away from Sunderland. (She probably thought it was 'abroad'.)

The sight of my grandfather sipping water from a light-blue plastic cup covered with a lid so he could hold it without spilling, and my father's obvious distress, still pains me. A few weeks later he was mercifully dead.

As an out-of-work engineer in the early 1930s, he was so hard up my father didn't have a single toy to play with and had to improvise by playing toy motor cars with his dad's shoes. My father told that story to me once in one of his 'you don't know how lucky you are' moments. I laughed so hard he never told it again.

Our first home was an old, end-of-terrace house, heated only by a coal fire. Condensation froze on the inside of the windows, creating fascinating snowflake patterns. This, along with the dark, mysterious air-raid shelter in the back yard, where my father kept his paint tins, and being scooped up by my panicking mother as I tried to crawl down a steep flight of stairs, are my only memories of 33 Merle Terrace.

I realise this may seem like abject poverty to some now, but in 1960s Sunderland, it was very much the norm. The

'60s never swung in Sunderland. I remember the 'summer of love' in 1967, seeing the long-haired hippies strumming guitars on Seaburn beach. Except the 'hippies' were muscular, with tattoos and the telltale blue-black scars on their backs and arms where coal dust had lodged in cuts as they crawled along narrow seams down the mines. Even to my young eyes, the incongruity struck me.

There was very little sign of the great cultural liberation sweeping the country. If the strains of the Beatles or Rolling Stones could be heard, it would be from an old valve wireless inside one of the thousands of humble workers' cottages. Maybe wafting through a scullery window and into the cobbled back lane where baggy-trousered youths kicked bald tennis balls against a wall, scoring a goal every time they hit the small wooden coal hatch. Everywhere was steeped in the grimy modesty of heavy industry.

As well as the scarred backs, there were other ways of spotting a coal miner in 'civvies'. In the outlying pit villages, the older men who had hewn coal for forty years would crouch down on their haunches as they drank their beer outside pubs or chatted in the park. These unique circular, hunched gatherings were a legacy of a lifetime spent working three-foot seams. Their clothes were famously gaudy too, the odd dash of yellow here or orange there to compensate for a life in darkness. And many had a passion for pigeon fancying or leek growing. Above the soil, miners craved colour and serenity.

They were tough men, too. One of the toughest boys I

knew played centre forward for a local team, Roker Boys, which acted as a feeder team for Sunderland AFC. As a midfielder, I played alongside him and watched with admiration his strength and physical prowess and how he dominated the field, a man among boys.

A couple of years later I bumped into him in one of the town's pubs. He'd gone down the pit and, although muscular and robust, looked a shadow of his former self. His cheeks were sallow and sunken, his back slightly bent and he was already coughing badly through the coal dust. He was twenty but looked forty. I asked him how he was and how the job was going. My old friend, who had proved so fearless when boots and elbows were flying around on the football pitch, was frank and honest. 'Everyone thinks we go down there in white overalls these days. I'm working a two-foot six-inch seam in three inches of water and it's f****** awful!'

The left can say what they like about Thatcher closing the pits. I never met a miner who wanted his son to follow him to the pithead.

My father, Tom, was a part of this industrial landscape. He was head of what is now called human resources but was then known as personnel management, working for Bristol Siddeley Engines, Rolls-Royce and David Brown, who made the gears for tractors as well as the Aston Martin. He ended up as the north-west regional director for Community Task Force, a part of the old government Manpower Services Commission.

Thanks to my father's professional progress and my mother

Audrey's long hours as a nurse and later a social worker, we ended up moving to an upmarket part of town in Barnes and later to a large Victorian house in Ashbrooke, considered the nicest part of town.

I started the chapter with the notion of the 1960s being one of 'genteel poverty' for my family. The poverty, or at least the relative poverty by today's standards, contrasted sharply with another part of the family history.

My mother's family had lived on the south banks of the Wear for generations. My maternal great-grandmother, Margaret Graham, was a formidable businesswoman. By the 1910s she had amassed a property fortune consisting of a whole street of houses in one part of Sunderland and half a street of houses in another. She also owned a chain of grocery stores.

They had enough money to give all their numerous sons, daughters and grandchildren smart houses for wedding presents. And my great-grandfather retired to the life of a gentleman aged just forty.

However, death duties and their largesse, coupled with the chronic asthma that plagued my family and made several bed-ridden and dependent, meant the fortune slowly dwindled. By 1949, the Attlee Labour government had taxed a lot of hard-working entrepreneurs out of existence with a top-rate band of an eye-watering 98 per cent. This meant for every pound they earned, they were allowed to keep the princely sum of 3d (2p).

By 1961, when I came along, this vast fortune had dwindled significantly. My parents were provided a home by my grandparents, but it was the humble terraced home in the shadow of the shipyard crane jibs.

I frequently joke that when anyone dies, I get the old watch. I've no idea where the cash goes to! The last relatively wealthy Graham to go west was my dear old aunt Edna, who died childless and left her entire estate to an osteoarthritis society. The only thing I managed to retrieve among the old family heirlooms and artefacts was my great-uncle's First World War medals. And then I had to technically steal them from the house before the charity got their hands on them and auctioned them off for buttons.

Great-grandmother Graham was a magnificent northern matriarch by all accounts. She died from heart failure aged sixty-four in 1934. A symptom of her illness in the last stages was apparently a bloated appearance due to extreme water retention. This caused my grandmother, her daughter, to describe her fatal illness to me as a boy as 'drowning in her own waters', which I thought sounded intriguingly horrific. Why 'waters' had to be plural, I still have no idea.

Not many people are remembered three generations down the line. But my great-grandmother is still spoken of with reverence even by the fourth. Flowers are still placed on the family grave in Sunderland even though she has been dead eighty years.

I was educated in the local state schools and formed many very happy friendships there that endure to this day. My secondary education was at the same school as my father – Bede

School. This was an old-style grammar school turned comprehensive. Some teachers still wore gowns, the cane was liberally used and it had the best reputation in the town, if not the county. Gradually, its status was eroded by the conversion to a comprehensive school. And in the 1990s, the narrow-minded socialist council that has blighted Sunderland's growth and improvement for generations turned it into a sixth-form college. I later learned from a council member that this was because many of the Labour councillors who had failed to pass the eleven-plus entrance exam were embittered and envious. This inverted snobbery is rife in Sunderland and is almost an inherited disease.

As my family moved back into relative prosperity, I was labelled a 'poshy' by certain boys. My accent didn't help either. My mother's side of the family were all well-spoken and I lacked the harsh north-eastern twang that signified masculinity and toughness. I also wore my hair neatly parted, shined my shoes and wore my collar fastened and my tie in a Windsor knot, which I fancied looked more 'sophisticated' but I imagine made me look rather a pretentious prat, and I was always treated as an outsider – a situation I have come to realise is probably my natural habitat. Fortunately, I was strong enough to fend for myself and was never bullied, but if I had been less robust, I would have been a prime candidate.

Playing for the football team also helped. I was a fairly decent midfielder and that way became quite pally with some of the toughest boys in the school, who occupied all the other positions on the team. 1973–80 were extremely happy years. I made many, many friends and see them all still. In fact, I still go on annual jaunts to France with several of them. A couple I've known since primary school in 1966. They are quite simply my dearest friends.

My parents were extremely liberal and I was encouraged very early on to break free from the apron strings. I started work aged twelve in 1974, delivering newspapers underage, morning and night, six days a week, for £1 (£1.15 if no incorrect deliveries were made!). This seemed to me to be slave labour, so after a few weeks, I wrote to the local car dealer and asked if I could help wash his fleet of thirty-plus cars that stood on a forecourt. So, for the princely sum of £1.50, I worked from 10 a.m. to 5 p.m. on Saturdays. In the summers, I worked on a farm nearby and another in Weardale, helping to bring in the hay from dawn till dusk for £6 a day and learning to shoot rabbits with the farmer's gun and drive his tractor. Incredible to think I was only thirteen. The farmer would be jailed today!

I left home for university in September 1980. Getting to university was a minor miracle as I had messed around with my A level subjects to a reckless extent, starting off with history, politics and, bizarrely, biology. However, after several months, I decided that matters such as the reproductive cycle of the amoeba had failed to grip me and so I switched to economics.

But at the end of the lower sixth, bored by the Marxist soliloquies of the master, I ditched economics for English just two weeks before the end-of-year exams. Unsurprisingly, I managed an embarrassing 26 per cent, prompting W. K. Lewis to remark on my report, 'Thurlbeck must seriously consider where his advantages lie.'

The following year, I had to cram two years into one, keeping up with the second-year syllabus while teaching myself the first year – including the heaviness of Milton and Chaucer.

Coupled with my self-inflicted burden was my complete reluctance to attend school at all. Weeks would go by without my making an appearance. Between January and Easter 1980, the staff had all but given up on me. Two weeks before the final exams, I crammed as much as I could, spouted it out and did well enough to satisfy the grade requirements for the universities in Manchester, Lancaster, Hull and Birmingham, and take the Bede School Rotary Prize for English.

My tolerant and encouraging English mistress, Mrs Pamela Atkinson, was my saving grace. I deserved to be slung out. But, instead, she wrote me a glittering testimonial which had impressed the four universities to such a degree, they all made me a conditional offer of a place without even asking me to interview.

I had jettisoned Hull and Birmingham as being too dull. And an eagerness to escape the urban griminess of Sunderland made me opt for Lancaster, which was close to my beloved Lake District, where I was to read English with the same haphazard approach as I did at school.

Before I left home, I sent Mrs Atkinson a bunch of flowers and a short note expressing my gratitude and thanks for having faith in such a wretch as I. She was a deep and thoughtful young woman, prone, as many deep and thoughtful young people are, to depression. She was also sensitive and shy. But she had the strength and independence of mind to ignore her superiors and refused to pigeonhole me as an idle loafer, and for that I will always be grateful to her. Four years ago, when I returned to my school to give a journalism lecture, I was distressed to learn of her death in her early sixties. An Old Bedan herself, she was a gifted teacher and I will be for ever in her debt.

My appearance at Lancaster got off to a flying start in the first year. A First in Theatre Studies and 2:1s in English and Philosophy. My portrayal of Jimmy Porter in Osborne's *Look Back in Anger* also got me a First in my drama practical and, at 76 per cent, it was the highest mark in the year.

By now I had decided that drama was far more interesting than poring over a lot of Old Norse, Anglo-Saxon poetry and medieval literature. Accordingly, I decided to opt out of any pretension of having any scholarly leanings whatsoever and aim low. The exciting life of the wandering troubadour held its charms. And, to some extent, I've been governed by its itinerant principles ever since.

As an active member of the university theatre group and the Theatre Studies department, I took part in back-to-back plays for the next two years, leaving virtually no time for study. In April 1982, the Theatre Studies professor Tom Lawrenson died. He and I had been drinking Scotch into the small hours during the Easter vacation. Only after the best part of a bottle had been consumed did he tell me he was having his cataracts removed under general anaesthetic the following day and he had been warned not to drink the night before. Sadly, Tom died on the operating table from a severe stroke.

Professor T. E. Lawrenson was a founding father of Lancaster University in 1964, when he had originally been professor of French and one of the most revered academic figures in Europe. His memorial service in June was to be attended by leading academics from as far afield as Australia and the university decided to put on a play at the Nuffield Theatre in his honour and to entertain the eminent visitors, his students and the staff.

In a nod to Tom's French scholastic backgound, Molière's *Le Malade Imaginaire* was chosen, although performed in English. And the performance was to be marked as our Theatre Studies practical examination, which I was studying as a minor. I auditioned for the lead role of Argan and got it. I based the performance on my old politics master at school, Mr W. Fell. Bill Fell was an old Bedan and an old bachelor with a fussiness and unintentional line in comic hypochondria, which turned his lessons into a Whitehall farce. Perfect for the self-obsessed Argan. I'd frequently amused my friends at Bede with my impersonation of Bill Fell and the Theatre Studies department thought it would be funny too. Thanks to Bill, I got top marks in the year for a second year in a row, scoring 81 per cent and another First.

Lest I leave the impression that Bill Fell was in any way a foolish man, he was in fact a man of extraordinary brilliance. After leaving Bede as a multi-prizewinner, he took a Double First in history at Oxford during the early 1940s. In 1970, he completed a politics degree at Durham University in just a year instead of the usual three – taking a First. In his long career of teaching A level politics, he had just one failure. He was the most loved and respected schoolmaster I've ever come across. He is now no longer with us. But even his demise had its own academic comedy, with him believing in the end that he was in fact the Edwardian Liberal Prime Minister Henry Campbell-Bannerman. Lesser minds tend to opt for Napoleon. God bless you, Bill.

Playing opposite me in the play, as my maid Toinette, was a beautiful young woman with a mass of wavy brown curls and huge green eyes. I'd known her since 1964, when we were at Miss Richie's nursery school together. She attended the local private Church High School for Girls, where I'd dated a few of her classmates, and I'd bumped into her at parties. Then she came to my sixth form to study for her A levels. On my first day at Lancaster, there she was again on my course and we became very good friends. She was frequently homesick and she felt like I was an older brother, and we laughed a lot too. We became extremely close but there was no question of us forming a relationship. We both had partners. I had a steady girlfriend from school who was at Liverpool University and she was dating one of my chums at Lancaster.

In 1987, four years after leaving Lancaster, a friend of hers passed me her number so I rang out of the blue and invited her for a drink. Another coincidence. She too had become a journalist. At Lancaster, I had always regarded her as my little sister. But standing before me was one of the most beautiful young women I'd ever seen. A petite size eight and with a heart-melting smile. Even though I'd known her since we were three years old, it had taken me until now to fall in love with her. And I did so on the very spot. In a little pub in Hampstead, where I lived. Within ten minutes, I had decided I would marry her. I proposed a few months later in a dingy guest house in the New Forest and, happily, she accepted.

We married in her old school church in February 1993 and a few months later our daughter Kate was born, followed by Phoebe five years later. 'Boo' and 'Bee', as they are known, have provided us with the happiest days of our lives. As my daughters get older, I preside over them with decreasing levels of influence. Alarmingly, my Christmas present from fourteen-year-old Bee this year was a cook's apron emblazoned with the slogan 'Prick with a fork'. There has always been a healthy disregard for authority in my family!

I had a wonderfully happy time at Lancaster. But I was never the most studious of pupils and my studies began to suffer. Shockingly, I only attended two lectures in three years and barely a handful of seminars. My tutors were despairing. To make matters worse, I did my usual absurdity of changing courses at the last minute, switching from single English honours to a joint English/Theatre Studies degree, which meant I had to cram two years into one. The decision just compounded the confusion and they could only award me a third.

I owed the library a fine of £3.50 and under the university rules they withheld my result until I paid it. I was so disinterested (I had started a job the day after my last exam in June 1983), I didn't bother to pay and find out my degree result for five weeks. In fact, it was my father who paid it for me. This was a shameful episode and one which I regret to this day. My parents deserved much better from me and I still feel I let them down. I tell the story to illustrate how infuriatingly self-confident I was in those days. I really believed I could make a big splash in the world on my own and on my own terms. I was foolishly rebellious and possessed of an arrogance which wasn't justified or attractive. I'm lucky to have kept all my friends.

I'm not one for self-psychoanalysis and I am not entirely certain what makes me so outwardly conventional and conservative and yet so absurdly hyper-independent and rebellious. The seeds of this contradictory nature might lie in my background. I am a mish-mash of old-fashioned, well-heeled middle-class entrepreneurs and mid-twentieth-century working-class street fighters. I belong to neither one nor the other. At school, I was never accepted as 'one of the regular boys'. I was classed as a strong-willed, 'posh' eccentric. In the East India Club, I think I'm regarded as a brash, self-made northerner.

We never really know ourselves fully. But I am certain that

I am very much an outsider and a loner. Even among my close circle of friends who I've known since I was five years old, I am the one who is ever so slightly on the periphery. Always last to make contact or be contacted and, in the 1980s, disappearing for years on end before strolling back.

On the *Today* newspaper, I was quickly pigeonholed by the news desk as a reporter to peel off from the rest of the Fleet Street pack to dig around on my own for an exclusive. On the *News of the World*, I worked alone and with very little guidance for the best part of two decades.

There were very few careers open to a man who was brash, pushy to the point of being aggressive, overly self-confident and armed with a third-class degree from a second-class university. Even fewer to one who couldn't abide authority figures or take orders from anyone but himself.

At university, the only thing I excelled at was acting, gaining extremely good notices in the college and regional press and never anything less than a First in practical exams. Everything was on course for drama school and the stage. But while several of my contemporaries advanced in this direction (most notably Andy Serkis of Gollum fame and my close friend David Verrey, who went to the RSC and the National Theatre), I did my usual trick of changing the game plan at the last minute. I took my final bow in 1983, washed off the panstick, got my final First and never set foot on a stage again.

It was an odd and unexpected decision. But something my father had told me as a boy still resonated. Dad was a superb singer, possessed of a wonderful, light tenor voice. Coupled with his brilliantined good looks, immaculate dress sense and aura of debonair charm and bonhomie, he enjoyed success as a dance band crooner after the war. In 1952, while still nineteen, he made a record with the RAF Dance Band, 'I'm Yours'. He sings it beautifully and I still have the original 78rpm record and it is the only recording I have of his voice at all. A picture of him in uniform singing into a large microphone looks down on me in my study.

Geraldo, the famous band leader, invited my dad to sing with his world-famous band. Although few under sixty will have heard of Geraldo now, this was rather like being invited to sing with One Direction today, or to duet with Robbie Williams. (Although, in those days, nowhere near as lucrative. The band leader took the royalties and paid his musicians and singers a simple living wage.)

Dad was tempted, of course. But he figured that living out of a suitcase all his life, 'with no pension at the end of it', was not a life for him. So he walked off that recording stage in 1952 and never sang commercially again. With hindsight, it was a sound decision. By 1955, the dance bands were no more, replaced by rock 'n' roll. And Dad was no Elvis Presley! Geraldo managed to limp on as a cruise ship dance band until the early 1970s but the glory days of million-selling recordings were no more.

That recording is, of course, my most precious possession. By the time I married in 1993, he'd been dead four years, felled by an unexpected heart attack after a lifetime of robust health, aged just fifty-six. I still miss him and think of him every day.

But I was lucky to be able to play his record for the first dance at my wedding reception in Lumley Castle, Co. Durham, where many of his friends listened with tears in their eyes as my dad crooned the lyrics of 'I'm Yours' and his son danced the foxtrot with his new bride.

I briefly took the microphone to introduce my father's record, ending with, 'Take it away, Dad,' and as I did, I registered briefly a look of puzzlement on the faces of his lifelong friends. Afterwards, I learned that none of them had any idea of his early singing career, such was his impeccable modesty. Only his mother had ever played the record. Over and over again, of course, as – like most women who knew my dad – she totally adored him, calling him her 'little chun boy'. I still have no idea what a 'chun boy' is. I only hope it isn't now something horribly racist!

So, like my father, I turned my back on the idea of settling into a show-business career. After three years of considering nothing else, I pulled off my usual routine. I threw everything up in the air and decided to try something else.

In 1984, I was living in the Lancashire mill town of Galgate with my girlfriend from university and I picked up a copy of *The Guardian* and turned to the situations vacant pages in the education section. The Sudanese Ministry of Education was looking for English teachers and we thought we'd apply.

Sudan was and still is a hostile country, ripped apart by civil wars and famine, and with a climate like no other. I recalled Alistair Cooke describing the climate on the radio once and his words had remained. 'There may be hotter places in the world than Khartoum. But if there is, I don't want to go there.'

By the summer of 1984, the famine which had decimated Ethiopia had swept into the Sudan and Chad, killing millions. Disease was rife and civil war was raging.

I was to be a sixth-form English master at a boys' boarding school in a village about 120 km south of Khartoum called El Hosh, and my girlfriend would teach in the girls' school. Our salary was the equivalent of £26 a week, which was roughly the same as we would have got on the dole in the UK. But in the Sudan, it put us in the top one per cent of salary earners.

We were met by a Sudanese teacher who showed us to our accommodation, assuring us as we walked that it was in fact 'the best house in the village'. In truth, when we got there, it looked no more than two garages joined together with chicken wire for windows. But compared to the rest of the village, it was luxurious. Many of the villagers lived in shacks. Many lived in communities of mud huts.

We had a small, walled yard where the ground had been scorched hard by the sun. Two electric lights. One cold tap in the yard, which, at head height, also doubled as a 'shower'. The lavatory was a hole in the ground at the bottom of the yard. And there were no mod cons. No TV, washing machine or cooker. Fortunately, we had come with a short-wave radio so it was possible to tune in to the BBC World Service, which was a godsend.

Washing, ironing, cooking and cleaning was carried out by a team of four maids, one for each job, as each task was a long labour in itself. And for their efforts, I paid them the equivalent of 10p a day. To pay a penny more would have incurred the anger of the villagers, as it would have led to increased wage demands elsewhere.

Washing had to be done by hand using a bar of soap in a three-foot washing pan the shape of a dinner plate. The drying was easy – clothes would be bone-dry and semi-bleached by the sun in minutes. A saturated towel would dry in fifteen minutes. My hair would dry on the 30-yard walk between the tap and our home.

Ironing was also labour intensive. There were no electric irons in the Sudan. Instead, hot charcoal was poured into primitive irons in much the same way our great-grandmothers used coal irons until the early 1920s.

Cooking had to be done on a small charcoal stove about twelve inches high and made from clay. There was just one ring to cook an entire meal. There were power cuts for days or weeks at a time, so candles were generally in use when the sun set at 6 p.m., which it did all year round. No electricity also meant no tap water, as the village pump ceased to work. A small earthenware pot, known as a 'zir', was constantly filled for emergency rations. In such cases, bathing with precious water became impossible and a 'sand bath' was used – handfuls of sand being rubbed across the body as a primitive exfoliant.

Food was scarce as the famine swept west from Ethiopia.

Lentils one day, ful masri (Egyptian beans) the next, the occasional rotten tomato, and rice and bread peppered with grit. On starvation rations and with the chronic bacterial and amoebic dysentery which stuck me down with grim regularity, my weight plummeted.

Malaria was a killer in the area among the undernourished, especially young children. Mothers frequently appeared at the house or the school, holding a limp child and begging for anti-malarial chloroquine tablets, which I had in abundance. We doled them out like Smarties, fully expecting to be able to buy or bribe our way back into supplies with our 'considerable' salary.

When they finally ran out, I discovered none were available. The result was instant malaria, so I self-medicated as best I could with black tea and rest.

Teaching the boys in the Sudan wasn't too hard. As it had been a British colony, English was a strong second language. And until the year before, when President Gaafar Nimeiry introduced strict Sharia law, it had been the language of teaching in all the schools. Even chemistry was taught in English.

Almost all the boys were Muslims and although they were boarders, their families all lived within a few hours' drive from the school. But two or three Christian boys came from the south of the country and were totally isolated from their families. A trip home would take several days and was only affordable once a year.

Peter Malek Aywell and John Deng were two such boys and

they regularly came to my home for free private tuition in English literature. They were from the very primitive Dinka tribe who were noted for their bravery and ferocity in battle. Peter and John were both over seven feet tall, which isn't unusual among the Dinkas. Their faces were almost a purplish-black with scars carved into their heads and faces – the straight lines denoting their unflinching bravery while self-inflicting the wounds with a sharp knife. They were also as bright as any boy I had studied with. I taught Peter chess and after a dozen or so games, he was beating me. They also loved the short-wave radio and listened to the BBC avidly. Peter couldn't listen to it without clutching it and resting it on the end of his knees!

Their visits were at their request and had soon become as much of a social gathering as anything. They were twenty-one (families had to save long and hard to send boys to school and students were often quite old) and I was twenty-two, so we were contemporaries and soon became good friends.

At school, class sizes were never below sixty, with five or six boys often sharing one textbook. There was no glass in the windows, causing sand to blow everywhere. And there were no teaching aids apart from a blackboard and chalk.

Sudan in 1984 was frozen in time. The former colony was granted independence in 1956, but the institutions which the British had installed remained and were largely unmodernised and falling into various states of disrepair. Steam trains still puffed along railway lines built by Kitchener at the end of the nineteenth century. Fuelled by charcoal, rather than the vastly superior coal, they barely exceeded 30mph. The most modern aeroplane was Sudan Airways' ageing, second-hand 707s, reserved for long hauls. But many internal flights were carried out by ancient 1930s German Fokker biplanes with room for just thirty passengers. Alarmingly, they would leave a trail of thick black smoke pouring from their propellers as they droned through the air.

I never came across a home with a telephone. Calls were all made from the local post office and had to be booked in advance. My call to my parents in England had to be arranged two weeks before I wanted to make it. So we resorted to letters, which took six weeks to arrive.

Even the machinery of government was of a bygone era. At the Ministry of Education in Khartoum, they still had a vast typing pool of about 400 women, all in serried rows, methodically clattering out bureaucratic missives on shiny black, 1920s Imperial typewriters.

And the most popular mode of travel was on foot. Followed by donkey. Only the wealthiest could afford cars, the most popular model being the 1950s Hillman Minx.

When I washed up at home in the spring of 1984, unannounced, my father answered the door. When he opened it he stood in the doorframe looking blankly at his only son. Although it had only been a year since he had last seen me, he didn't recognise me. My face was tanned and my hair was bleached by the Sudanese sun. But I had become unrecognisable due to my chronic weight loss. I stood on the bathroom scales. When I left the UK, I was 11st 6lbs. I was now 8st 10lbs. Even my muscles had wasted through illness and chronic food shortages. At 5ft 11in., I was skeletal.

Over the years, I've had a couple of trips to hospital or the doctor to deal with recurrent malaria. Both bouts hit me when I was on holiday, allowing me to maintain my family tradition of no Thurlbeck taking a day off work sick since 1915. The only other side effects are a propensity to tan in the merest blink of sunshine and an inclination to carry more weight in case I'm forced to face a starvation diet again. I have been 13 stone since I was twenty-five – about a stone overweight. But compared to the suffering of the Sudanese, through drought, famine, civil war, bullets, shrapnel and shell, I count myself lucky.

Despite the privations, the Sudan was a golden opportunity for adventure and for making contacts and plans. Some of the contacts I made during my travels I remain in touch with to this day. And my plan, on my return to England, was to become a journalist.

CHAPTER 2

TO THE *HARROW OBSERVER*

I **N 1985, I** was twenty-three years old and if I was to become a journalist, I had to start making tracks quickly.

The best opportunities were and still are in London. In the early '80s, the best newspaper journalism route was through the training scheme of the now defunct Westminster Press, which owned dozens of the best local and regional newspapers in the UK.

If you were lucky enough to be taken on by one of their newspapers, they would pay your salary while you underwent an intensive training course at their college in Hastings, East Sussex. Here, young indentured trainees learned reporting skills, journalism law and the workings of local and central government.

After five months, the fledgling hacks would return to their papers to undergo two years of on-the-job training before they were taken on as full-time members of staff.

It was a luxury now long since vanished. Newspapers now demand their new reporters arrived fully formed, having financed themselves through college to win journalism 'qualifications' and acquire 'skills' learned from a big fat book, which seems to me half the use, twice the price and a fraction of the fun.

Places on these courses were rare, however. There were two intakes of twenty to twenty-five each per year. Of the dozens of newspapers across the country, each paper only took on a new trainee once every year or two. And each place was fiercely contested. Newspaper offices were inundated with hundreds of CVs from new graduates desperate to get a foothold in journalism.

I was fortunate that I got on extremely well with my girlfriend's parents and they very kindly allowed us to live with them in their home in Harrow, Middlesex while I searched for my first job in journalism.

The next intake was January 1986, so a job of any sort was vital to pay my way through the next half year. A few weeks later, I found myself a position as a personnel manager at the head office of Homebase on a three-month temporary contract. When that ended, I moved to Tesco's, increasing my salary from £6,500 to £9,500 p.a.

But, while my accidental career in human resources flourished, my first steps into journalism looked bleak. You will never see an advert saying, 'Trainee journalist required, apply within.' Newspapers rely on candidates showing initiative.

Bizarre as it may sound, many harbouring ambitions to be a journalist are put off at the first hurdle – they simply don't know the route map.

So I sent off twenty-two speculative applications. Over the next few weeks, twenty-one replies came back, all saying they had no vacancies, either now or in the foreseeable future. The *Harrow Observer* replied, offering me a glimmer of hope, saying a vacancy may turn up in the next few months and they would keep my application on file.

A few months later, I wrote back reminding them and asked if we could meet for a conversation. The editor, Nick Carter, asked me to submit two written pieces of no more than 500 words each on the subjects of 'The person I most admire' and 'Journalism's role in society' and he would get back to me.

After a few days, he wrote back asking me to attend an 'interview and exam' day in the newspaper office. Twenty applicants had been shortlisted to undergo a series of aptitude tests and interviews lasting a full Saturday. We were given an IQ test and mock interviews to write up, and were grilled by the editor, deputy editor and news editor. I thought I'd given a decent account of myself but feared the odds were stacked against me. Too much competition. And there were a couple of local applicants too, who always had a big advantage. And everyone had good university degrees, some shinier than others!

Two weeks later, the phone rang in my office. It was Nick Carter with the simple words I'll never forget: 'We'd very much like you to join our team.'

After gratefully accepting, I put down the receiver and walked across the office and into the staff canteen for a cup of tea. I felt as though I was floating two inches above the carpet, such was my elation. To date, that moment is still among the happiest of my whole life.

This was my first real career break after the grim horrors of the Sudan and the drudgery and boredom of human resources.

By now, I had quickly progressed through the salary grades in my ill-suited office job and was earning almost £12,000 p.a., a decent sum for a 23-year-old in 1986.

I later learned this was what swung Nick's decision in my favour. I'd been up against some extremely able applicants, he explained. But none could beat me for commitment. 'Why anyone would want to chuck in a salary of £12,000 for £6,700 was beyond me. You were neck and neck with best. But you stood out as the one who could demonstrate you wanted the job more than anyone else.'

I have an awful lot to be grateful to Nick Carter for. An avuncular son of a diplomat, he encouraged and nurtured his staff like the very best of editors. And he gave me my first break in journalism. Even when the odds are stacked against me, I have always been lucky. My family have always called me 'Lucky Jim'. And I was lucky to meet Nick Carter that day.

At the college in Hastings, there were twenty-six of us on the five-month course and seven of us would end up occupying quite senior roles on national newspapers in the coming years. One of them was Andy Coulson.

Andy was a nineteen-year-old trainee for the *Basildon Evening Echo* in Essex and straight out of sixth form. My first impression of him was that he was quiet and very laid-back but with a very strong sense of self-confidence. But it was a natural self-confidence, not one which irritated or jarred through lack of talent. He was focused, shrewd, clever and very diligent. He was also very sensible. He was never seen taking part in any high jinks and was never tipsy, let alone raucously drunk. He was also extremely adept at getting on with absolutely everyone and careful not to belong to a clique. These were all the talents which very quickly marked him out as rock-solid management material by News International.

Although we were never close friends, we got on very well and I liked him. I admired his blasé decision to dump any idea of going to university and simply get on with the real task he had set himself so early in life – becoming a newspaper journalist. He was one of just two or three on the course without a degree. But he quickly outshone most of them and I respected him for that.

Driving around in his second-hand Ford Cortina (with a kitsch furry cover on the gear lever), he had some of the archetypal Essex boy about him, which never entirely fell away. I used to gently rib him for it. He, in turn, used to spread the story that whenever you visited Nev at his digs, he was always boiling fish and listening to Cole Porter! He turned up at my digs freezing one day and I donated him one of my old overcoats and watched as he shuffled off down the back lane in the driving rain – the future Prime Minister's spokesman in a battered tweed coat belonging to my late grandfather!

Andy sat at the back of the class, taking in everything and rarely pushing himself forward. When he did make a contribution to a discussion, it was considered and relevant. Andy was a classic old head on young shoulders, the sort of person who makes a good head boy in a good state school.

Nearly twenty years later, when I came to be his news editor and then chief reporter, he was essentially the same man – although his leadership qualities had become more highly developed and he had acquired the tendency of every Fleet Street editor to fly off the handle occasionally! But he was essentially the same decent man whom I'd first met in 1986. Nothing will ever persuade me that Andy Coulson is anything other than a fundamentally good man. And he's one of the best journalists and finest editors I have ever worked with.

Newspaper newsrooms in the 1980s were vastly different to the ones today. Mechanical typewriters thundered in unison at deadline time with a sound like an express train. As the final deadline approached, ringing telephones would add to the frantic cacophony with their urgent, trilling bells. The noise would be so loud, reporters would have to shout down the phone to their contacts. And to be heard, the contact would have to yell back down the line.

Reporters often smoked and left their cigarettes smouldering in ashtrays as they hugged the phone between shoulder and ear while they typed at the same time. Ageing sub-editors, who measured and laid out pages using an em rule and a pencil, added to the fug with pipes and untipped Senior Service cigarettes. Reporters typed stories in triplicate using carbon paper with just one sheet per paragraph. Photographers developed their pictures with chemicals in dark rooms. Everyone drank beer for lunch. And it was gloriously chaotic.

My very first job was to go to Downing Street to pick up a copy of the New Year Honours list on 2 January 1987. The editor telephoned the press office and told them to expect me. My memory of the event illustrates how much the world has changed in just twenty-eight years. There were no gates at the end of the street then and I sauntered down the footpath to the famous black front door, so shiny I was able to see my reflection to straighten my hair. A policeman in ordinary uniform, with no machine gun or bulletproof protection, stood like an affable Dixon of Dock Green next to it. I stood at the door. The policeman looked at me. I didn't know what to do. Did I knock on the door like I was calling on a school friend? Or would that cause an outrage? 'Good God! What do you think you're doing?! Go round the back, you idiot!'

So I asked the policeman's advice. Without even asking for proof of identity, he looked at me, smiled and said, 'Just knock on the door.' I knocked. A man dressed in a black coat and pinstriped trousers, whom I took to be a butler of sorts, answered. I told him my name and business and expected him to hand me the list. Instead, he said, 'Ah, yes, come in.'

I'd just walked up to the home of the British Prime Minister and the very epicentre of government, knocked on the front door and been told to 'Come in'. It was eccentrically English, I thought. He left me alone for a full five minutes in the front hall while he fetched the list. No body-scan or search. All that was to change for good in 1991 when the IRA launched a mortar attack on Downing Street, and the security around the Prime Minister is now among the tightest in the world.

We had the three weekly editions covering Harrow, Stanmore and Pinner, with eleven reporters in total. And in my first eighteen months, I had brought in the front-page splash sixty-three times. The management were extremely encouraging. Even though Westminster Press was a stuffy old outfit, they bent the rules and made me chief reporter after eighteen months when I was still a trainee.

For this rule-bending and promotion, I am eternally grateful to the news editor, Graham Newson. Graham is still one of the finest (and funniest) writers I have ever come across. And he taught me how to write too, just by watching him as he rewrote my copy on his typewriter. Every sentence stripped down to its bare essentials. One day at the start of my career, after a fatal gas explosion at the home of an elderly couple, I rambled on, trying to inject the necessary drama into a description of the scene in time for the following day's front page.

Graham – or 'Gammy', as he was known – read it and calmly deleted my 'dramatic' narrative, replacing it with the following two one-sentence paragraphs:

At 3.15 p.m., Mr Chaplin lit a match to make an afternoon cup of tea.

The blast rocked the street.

And there you have it. A perfect example of tabloid journalism at its very best. All the essential information conveyed in just nineteen words. All we need to know is in those short sentences. The causes and consequences. But also the drama, the horror, the tragedy and the pathos. The final five-word paragraph, standing powerfully alone. No need for any further explanation. We already know what happened to Mr Chaplin in that suburban Harrow street. I immediately realised this was a man I could learn from. And I absorbed everything he told me unquestioningly. He later went on to a have a very successful career with the BBC and has just retired. He is still one of my greatest friends.

It was a blissfully happy time. For the first time in my life, I felt I was doing something I was good at and would enjoy immensely. I threw myself into my new job and I felt I could handle everything thrown at me instinctively. I immediately knew this had been the right career choice and I worked every night building up contacts, meeting them in bars all over London.

I also loved Harrow, for all its Betjemanesque suburban ordinariness. I'd rented a little semi-detached house in Harrow Weald for £420 a month. Then I sub-let the rooms at a rent which more than covered my own rent too. So I lived rent-free in a comfortable little home. I also became very pally with some of my work colleagues and still count the deputy editor, Terry Payne, as among my dearest chums. They taught me an awful lot about the craft of journalism (for that is what it is – it's not a profession).

They marvelled at my ability to bring in front-page splashes week after week. At this point, I have a small confession to make. There was a very good reason why I seemed to magically produce a splash week after week for the paper. And it wasn't exactly by fair means.

In those pre-email days, the most onerous daily task for the news desk was to open a two-foot pile of letters every morning and assess them for story suitability.

We all had keys to the office and I used to let myself in at 8 a.m., a good hour and a half before the news team arrived. When 'Gammy' took his seat at around 9.30 a.m., he would find all the letters opened and in a neat pile on his desk awaiting his perusal – a kind of journalistic apple-for-the-teacher gesture.

Or so he thought! In fact, I would pinch the best stories of the week for myself and, armed with a breast pocket stuffed with splashes and page leads, scooped my colleagues week after week.

I worked flat out every day and evening. But it didn't seem like work as I enjoyed myself so much. I frequently brought in my own story ideas and searched for stories and interviews which interested me, in the firm belief that if they did, they would also interest the reader.

It also gave me the opportunity to seek out and interview people who interested me. One little task I set myself was to see which stage or screen star was appearing at the local theatres in that part of Middlesex. Then I'd look at their tour itinerary and hit the road in my ageing Volkswagen Beetle to review their show at the venue where they were performing prior to landing on my patch. Here, in some far-flung theatre, I would compose my review. But I would also secure a short interview with the star in question. The prospect of a feature in the local paper of the area where they were next to perform was always too good to miss. No one ever objected to my request for 'just ten minutes in the dressing room' before the show went up. It's amazing how many questions you can ask in ten minutes. And when you're in the door, it's amazing how ten minutes always morphs into twenty!

The two comic heroes who stand out in my memory are Norman Wisdom and Frankie Howerd. Norman was a delight, feigning being awestruck at being interviewed by 'the world-famous *Harrow Observer* – corr!' and demonstrating the dramatic pratfalls he would go on to perform well into his nineties. Frankie was just Frankie – the same off-screen as on. This time rowing with the telephone operator, 'Listen, missus, no, listen. I can't get through on the line, you see! What? Engaged? Here, I'm not a flaming lavatory you know!' And a memorable few minutes with Quentin Crisp. Why had he flaunted his homosexuality so colourfully in the 1930s? 'Dear boy, if the press were to start photographing people in public lavatories, don't build higher walls, simply learn to urinate in style.'

My salary soared to the unheard-of heights of £15,000 p.a. by 1989 as I muttered about wanting to move to a bigger paper. It seems such a pittance now but the chief reporter on weekly paid-for newspapers is lucky to earn that now, more than a quarter of a century later.

My social life blended seamlessly with my work life and I threw myself into both with great gusto. I had no responsibilities, no financial commitments and, as I had parted amicably from my girlfriend by now, no emotional ties.

But, like all young men, the gusto got the better of me one day, leading to the most bizarre series of events. After a one-night stand with an attractive young girl, we parted company early in the morning as I headed to a funeral. At the funeral tea, I came out in a rash all over my chest. Then down my back and arms and then all over my body. Small, itchy pin-pricks everywhere.

Back home, I consulted a book I'd been given to self-medicate while in the Sudan called *Where There Is No Doctor*. I went to the index and searched for 'itching'. And there it was, alongside a host of other probable causes: the word 'syphilis'.

It was 11 p.m. but I raced to Northwick Park Hospital A&E department, where a man behind a glass screen demanded to know what was wrong with me in front of about thirty other people in the waiting room.

'I think I might very well have syphilis,' I heard myself

saying, just loud enough to be heard through the glass but also by the entire waiting room. 'What symptoms?' asked the note-taker. By now, a few people were stifling giggles so I demanded to be seen in private by a doctor. I was shown into a room where a young female doctor, just out of college and on the graveyard shift, was working behind a desk. My embarrassment was compounded by the fact that she was the prettiest thing I'd ever seen, in a white coat with the whitest long blonde curls to match.

After examining me, there came an equally embarrassing series of questions.

'Do you know the girl?'

'No.'

'Can you contact her?'

'No.'

'Where does she work?'

'A teacher, I think.'

'Where?'

'Sorry, I don't know.'

She looked at me and tut-tutted. 'Surely you must have her phone number?' But I'd left in a hurry for the funeral and, in my haste, I'd forgotten even to do that.

She despatched me to the Martha and Luke Clinic in Hammersmith, what is known in street parlance as 'the clap clinic'. Inside, a lady who bore an uncanny resemblance to Mammy Two Shoes on the *Tom and Jerry* cartoons wielded a hooked syringe which she was determined to insert into a very delicate appendage to take a sample for the microscope. I nearly passed out with fear and before I relented, she had to follow me around the room as I backed off into various corners at speed.

The tests done, I waited a week for the results and was told to see my GP. 'Negative. Nothing wrong with you.' Huge relief. 'But what about the rash?' The doctor deduced: 'Well, the rash is where your socks, shorts, vest and shirt are. But not on your calves, knees or thighs. In other words, where you come into contact with the clothes you wash. What sort of detergent do you use?'

'Anything I put my hands on really,' I replied.

'How do you wash them?' I explained that as the house didn't have a washing machine, I just used to throw them in the bath and slosh them around, then rinse them in a bath of clean water. 'That's it, then,' said the doctor. 'You can't rinse clothes properly like that! You've got a rash from the detergent. Use the bloody launderette. Next!'

I was hugely relieved not to have caught something nasty. But I was also relieved that the embarrassment of it all had ended. Or so I hoped.

A few weeks later, I was at Harrow School, covering a public meeting for the paper. The school wanted to build a theatre in the school grounds, much to the annoyance of the locals, who had gathered in force to object. As I sat in the audience, out of the corner of my eye I spotted a beautiful young woman with flowing blonde curls. The doctor who had examined me. Oh, Lord! I sank back into my chair.

The meeting over, I repaired to the Castle pub nearby and was ordering a pint of beer when the blonde woman appeared from nowhere and smiled at me. I'm used to people sidling up to me hoping to get their name in the paper. But this was altogether different. I smiled back. I was desperate to tell her that I'd been given the all-clear and that I wasn't the bawdy sot she must have thought me.

'I got the all-clear, by the way.'

'What do you mean?'

'I got the all-clear from the Martha and Luke Clinic. I haven't got syphilis!'

Her smile began to fade. 'Sorry, have we met before?'

'Yes, yes! Of course. You examined me after I had that … er … dodgy one-night stand and I thought I had syphilis! It was the soap powder I use. Pah! Silly, eh? Ho, ho!'

By now she was backing off. 'Who do you think I am?'

'You're the doctor who examined my rash!'

Her smile had morphed into a sort of startled grimace with eyes and mouth wide open as she appeared to look around her for help.

'I most certainly am not! I'm the headmaster's secretary!'

In the next few months I was promoted first to news editor of the sister paper, the *Buckinghamshire Advertiser*, then to group features editor for all the company's papers in Middlesex, which included the *Harrow Observer*, *Wembley Observer*, *Uxbridge Gazette*, *Ealing Gazette* and the *Middlesex*

Chronicle. And I was still officially a trainee. But, as happy as those Harrow days were, I had already had a glimpse of the exciting life of a Fleet Street journalist and decided this was where my future lay.

In June 1988, I had investigated Harrow's main hotel – the Monksdene – which had a group of call girls running a vice den on the premises. Local dignitaries came and went and the scandal was about to sweep the sleepy suburban borough.

As we came off the presses, I picked up the phone to the *News of the World* and dictated the story to copytakers. Five minutes later, the assistant news editor, David Leslie, was on the phone to me. They wanted it. And could they have it exclusively, please. It duly ran as a page 3 lead that Sunday and he promised me £350 for my efforts. Would I be happy with that?

Seizing my opportunity and realising from David's tone of voice that £350 wasn't the bottom line, I agreed to the £350 on the condition that they give me two weeks of paid-for shifts to show them what I could do. David thought he'd got a bargain. But I realised I'd snatched the chance of a lifetime.

CHAPTER 3

TO FLEET STREET

FLEET STREET JOURNALISTS are hewn from the same stone but come in different shapes.

Fundamentally, we have the same set of skills and qualities and faults. We are all ultra-curious, anti-authoritarian, analytical, methodical, outgoing, confident, plausible, chameleon-like people. Able to talk to a titled aristocrat or a school dinner lady on a reasonably confident footing.

A *Daily Mail* reporter could fit as easily into *The Sun*, and they frequently do. So the newspaper we end up working for is a fairly random event. Journalists tend not to choose the paper they work for, the paper seems often to choose them. And so it was with me.

My scoop for the *News of the World* had me pigeonholed straight away as an undercover reporter who could work alone and pass himself off plausibly as someone else. And that is the way it remained for the rest of my career. The fact that my previous news editor Graham Newson had said I was the best feature writer he had come across counted for nothing now.

If you're lucky to find yourself selected from many other free-lance rivals jockeying for a position on a paper and bunged into a pigeon hole – into it you go.

My first day on the *News of the World* as a freelance was in June 1988. In Harrow, I'd been the proverbial big fish in the small pond. But walking up to the *News of the World* building in Wapping was daunting. My reputation as a big hitter on my local paper also counted for nothing. Everyone on Fleet Street had been big hitters on their local paper. And most of the big hitters didn't make the grade on Fleet Street and returned to the provinces. Of the tens of thousands of journalists in the UK, only a few hundred eventually make it as Fleet Street reporters.

Despite this, I had every confidence I would succeed. This may sound terribly arrogant but I assure you it isn't. It was a simple assessment of my own abilities here and lack of them there. I have already outlined what an appalling academic I was and how my early ambitions floated aimlessly. I also had a very real understanding of my own failures. But now I thoroughly believed I had yet to come across a journalist who could best me. And that belief continued with me for another twenty-three years on Fleet Street.

Despite this, I was very uptight and anxious as I took the lift to the top floor. I realised the *News of the World* was going to be vastly different to the *Harrow Observer*. But how different? Would all the reporters be demons? Would the newsroom be like Dante's Inferno, with flames shooting from the keyboards?

My experience was totally the opposite. I walked through

the door and introduced myself to the legendary news editor Bob Warren, who showed me to a desk. News editors, even on local papers, are ferocious types. But Bob, a former Royal Navy officer, was blessed with gentlemanly courtesy. The late Derek Jameson memorably described him as having the air of a public schoolmaster but with an encyclopaedic knowledge of the foibles of every scoutmaster in England.

The first reporter I met was Clive Goodman, the then royal correspondent, who introduced himself, shook my hand and took me to the canteen for a cup of tea and to explain the serious business of how to fill in an expenses form with maximum profit. Clive was a typical middle-class grammar schoolboy with a blazing line in caustic wit. An eccentric loner with a fondness for handmade suits and shoes, he cut a dash around the office and still holds the *News of the World* record for the most consecutive front-page splashes in a row: six. (I managed five.) I liked Clive a lot and despite his imprisonment after the 2006 royal phone-hacking scandal, still hold him in the highest professional regard. If that makes me unpopular with certain sections of the media and society in general, well, so be it.

The legendary investigator Trevor Kempson (the fake sheikh Mazher Mahmood's predecessor) was in full flourish. I had been reading his astonishing scoops since the early 1970s and he was a genuine, fully-fledged Fleet Street legend.

In 1973, he was responsible for the resignations of two Conservative ministers, Lord Lambton and Lord Jellicoe, after he caught them consorting with prostitutes. I had expected a tough street fighter with a dash of barrow boy in him. But while he was very strong-minded and determined (his motto was 'softly, softly, catchee monkey'), he was a Haberdashers' Aske's old boy and possessed of a kind of seedy glamour.

I struck up conversations with Trevor at every opportunity. How did he break the Lambton story? I was desperate to emulate his methods. Trevor explained he had concealed a small microphone in the nose of a teddy bear he had planted on the prostitute's bed. He had also paid the prostitute's husband to photograph the Air Minister *in flagrante* through a two-way mirror.

Trevor was very kind to me and took me under his wing, and for a while I acted as his 'bag-carrier', helping him out on stories. Occasionally, we'd have a drink in the old Printer's Pie in Fleet Street after work, then head off in his red, two-door Jaguar coupé to his flat in the Barbican to make some taped phone calls on investigations. During the course of a working evening like this with Trevor, he would drink whiskey like beer, pouring out half-pint tumblers. Bald and bespectacled, he had an unfortunate resemblance to the Nazi monster Adolf Eichmann when captured and put on trial in 1960. Despite this, his charm and wit made him very popular with women, and several stunning girlfriends in seductive poses adorned his walls.

Trevor died in the early 1990s, a victim not of his hard drinking but of leukaemia. I owe a lot to Trevor and his ability and willingness to share his skills with one so young and green as myself.

Also on the news desk were two formidable Ukrainians. Alex Marunchak was firm, direct yet taciturn and the most formidable news desk operator I've ever encountered. He had amassed a large volume of essential core contacts who fed the newspaper splash after splash, week after week. During his years as a crime reporter, Alex had made contact with policemen who would be most useful to him. He would sooner have a drink with a DC from London's West End than a chief inspector from Kent, calculating the DC would be better placed to give him a tip-off when a drunken A-lister was arrested on a Friday night after tumbling out of a louche nightspot.

Saturdays were the most stressful day of the week at the *News of the World*, as at all Sunday newspapers. Stories the news editor has been promising the editor all week can suddenly collapse. New angles to stories can be demanded at the very last minute and have to be obtained – especially if the editor has ordered them. In the middle of this, a big story might be breaking – a plane crash, an MP resigning, a celebrity dying, a brutal murder. The news editor needs to pull all the strands of every story together and present it fit for publication in the tensest situations and in a limited amount of time.

On press day, when the stories are going to bed on a big newspaper, it can feel like you are being fired at from all directions, as I was to find out in 2001, when I became news editor myself. Sub-editors would be demanding 'more copy', the editor would be angry as a favourite story collapsed, reporters making excuses for failing to deliver, awkward contacts suddenly pulling out of a deal to provide a story, or demanding unrealistic cash advances, a brilliant new source turning out to be a greedy fantasist.

Piers Morgan once told me that the hardest job in Fleet Street was that of news editor at the *News of the World*. It certainly takes a certain type of character. But one of the most vital qualities is the ability to remain calm under serious amounts of pressure. Marunchak was the master at this. When he was under severe pressure on the desk, the only visible symptom was his tendency to stroke his silver-grey moustache as he calmly, even coldly, dished out very precise, tightly worded orders that left you in no doubt what was needed and expected. I never heard him raise his voice once and yet he had total command over his troops and was feared and revered in equal measure. The same was said of Leonard Cheshire, who, as a squadron leader in the Second World War, led his fellow Halifax bomber pilots through flak and into the teeth of hell. An RAF veteran once told me, 'As he did so, all his fellow pilots could hear in their earpieces was Cheshire murmuring, "Lower, boys, lower please," as if he was dispensing a simple request from his fireside armchair.'

All successful leaders dealing with a crisis tend to be unflappable. And so it was with Alex. The shouting, screaming news executives who lose their cool and lose control tend to lose the dressing room and deepen the crisis. And this is what ultimately happened at the *News of the World* before its closure. But in the 1980s and 1990s, the culture at the *News of the World* was to treat staff with gentlemanly firmness. Firmness was essential, as a newsroom is jammed to the rafters with egos and very big personalities who, if you allow them to, will ignore you and do things their own way, believing they know best. But the management style was laced with respect, advice, assistance, precise direction borne from finely honed news sense, and instant feedback.

This type of management style was the hallmark of Bob Warren, who acted as news editor and assistant editor from 1964 until his death in 2009. And it was inherited by his successor Alex Marunchak, Alex's replacement Greg Miskiw (pronounced 'miss-cue'), and later, I hope, myself. In my two years as news editor, I never raised my voice once at any reporter. Nor did I bully or threaten anyone. I didn't need to. I had the best reporters in the tabloid world working for me. All I had to do was give them precise direction and off they went.

In 1988, the *News of the World* was selling more than 5 million copies every Sunday and was read by almost 15 million people. Taking children out of the equation, this meant the paper was read by about one in three of the reading population. It was a national institution and a phenomenally successful newspaper.

Week after week, the paper splashed stories that were eagerly awaited by the Saturday night news desks of every daily paper in the world. The anticipation would often boil over into a rumour frenzy, with an MP's non-appearance at a summer fête or a rock star cancelling a concert being interpreted as a signal they were about to be exposed for some scandalous affair or nefarious act in the *News of the World*. The false rumour would sweep Fleet Street, and our night desk phone would ring off the hook: 'We've heard you're exposing Joe Bloggs tomorrow. Can you give us a steer?'

With such a massive circulation came big revenues. It was often quoted that we made £1 million a week profit. Adjusted for inflation averaging 3.4 per cent a year since then, that works out at £2,270,000 a week.

The paper was so wealthy, in his early days Bob Warren didn't even have an editorial budget. He simply asked for the money to buy a story and it was given. Reporters enjoyed a five-star lifestyle. When working out of town, we were accommodated in the town's best hotel and every expense was billed back to the company – even the champagne. Despite this, expenses for £400 a week were still submitted and signed off.

Many reporters drove fast sports cars at the weekend, sent their children to private schools, employed nannies and cleaners and generally lived a racy lifestyle. My first salary as a humble starter at the paper was £40,000 a year. Twenty-odd years later, the starting salary on Fleet Street papers isn't much over £30,000.

Consequently, the competition for a job on the *News of the World* was the toughest on Fleet Street. After a year freelancing for them and working as deputy news editor on the *Western Mail* in Cardiff, I was on the verge of being offered a staff job when disaster struck.

The editor, Patsy Chapman, had got it into her head that I was a spy for the *Sunday Mirror*.

Sunday newspaper editors are always anxious about protecting their exclusives from rivals, and there had been some leaks. I was apparently spotted looking curiously over the shoulder of one reporter as he rattled out the following day's front-page splash. In the febrile paranoia, I instantly became chief suspect. I was unaware of it at the time, but she had insisted that the news desk got rid of me.

Patsy was becoming increasingly erratic and the news desk thought her aberration would pass. Greg Miskiw, Marunchak's deputy, came over and asked me to go to the Ford motor works in Dagenham, where a bomb had been found and isolated. Off I went. No bomb. I called Miskiw.

'There's no bomb, Greg.'

'Oh well, just go home then,' was the odd reply. It was just the start of my shift.

For six weeks I was given no work. Then, out of the blue, I was asked back into the office. But as soon as I sat down, Greg rushed over with the instruction to cover a demonstration outside the Chinese embassy following the Tiananmen Square massacre. But when I arrived, I saw my fellow reporter John Chapman was there too. I rang Greg.

'Do you realise Chapman is here too and you're double-handed here?'

'Oh, I didn't realise that. Just go home then,' came the baffling reply.

It would be five years before the *News of the World* would call me again and I would discover the reason why – that the news desk had hoped Patsy had forgotten all about me. She hadn't and blew a gasket when she saw me walking through the office. Although through it all, she said not one word to me.

A year of hard work had come to nothing and my Fleet Street career had juddered to a halt.

CHAPTER 4

TO THE
DAILY MIRROR

I F THE PERILOUS instability of Fleet Street life hasn't become apparent to you yet, the next few pages should put that right.

After more than a year of working Saturdays and holidays as a freelance at the *News of the World*, I felt isolated and depressed in my role as deputy news editor at the *Western Mail* in Cardiff. I had arrived at the Wales morning newspaper in February 1990 and found the place grim and dysfunctional, and most of the staff unhappy.

Looking back, I was bordering on being clinically depressed. I was posting letters into litter bins instead of pillar boxes and leaving my car keys in the door. All signs of a mind distracted.

Part of it was the gloominess then of the old *Western Mail* offices, where I was chained to my desk overseeing five regional editions a day. A hefty old broadsheet which swallowed thousands of words every day. And I had to read and check every one of them. It felt like being in charge of a sausage machine.

I desperately wanted to be on the road as a roving reporter and for a big national newspaper.

So one Monday morning, as I drove into work, I decided on the spur of the moment to hand in my notice the minute I walked through the door. And that is what I did. No job to go to. But I wouldn't get one sitting all day in an office in Cardiff.

It was August 1990 and Saddam Hussein's Iraqi Army had marched into Kuwait, precipitating an international crisis. All the newspapers were sending their London staff to military bases in Kuwait and Bahrain to cover the rising tensions. Sensing this would leave them depleted on the domestic front, I moved to explore the opportunity.

My contract said I had to give a month's notice. I told them I'd be gone in a week and advised them not to advertise but to appoint from within a talented reporter with aspirations to move onto the news desk.

Once again, I'd torn up the plan and thrown everything up in the air. I walked outside to have a drink with a former Fleet Street legend, Bill Cork, who was one of my staff. 'Corky' had been a big star on the Scottish *Daily Record* in the 1980s and had also worked on the *Daily Mirror* and the *News of the World* in London. A fine operator and possessed of a fine *joie de vivre*, he was crowned Scottish Reporter of the Year for talking prisoners into ending a violent prison siege. Bill had lost his pole position in Scotland as he became hooked on heroin, allegedly after being slipped some by a villain while working undercover. In an act of magnificent kindness, he handed me his contacts book, with the numbers of the great and the good – from Ronnie Biggs in Rio to Lauren Bacall and Bob Hope. He let me copy every entry and it was an extremely powerful tool to enter Fleet Street with. Bill became a very close friend and would turn up at my house with flowers for my wife and entertain everyone with his mischievous wit. He sadly died a few years later in his early forties, the result of an accidental heroin overdose after years of 'cold turkey'. I owe him a huge thanks.

After the drink with Corky, I then stepped outside into a telephone box, rang the *Daily Mirror* and told them I wanted five minutes with the news editor the following week to discuss something important. I wasn't going to mess around with letters and CVs, knowing the hundreds which cross a news editor's desk and end up in the bin. Fleet Street news editors wait until they see something different before replying.

I calculated they would be a little intrigued and that everyone can spare a mere 'five minutes', and my gamble paid off. The news editor, Steve Lynas, agreed to meet the following week.

In August 1990, the *Daily Mirror* was based in its iconic building on the corner of New Fetter Lane and Holborn Circus. I'd seen it on my London trips as a boy, emblazoned with the mastheads of the *Mirror*, the *Sunday Mirror* and *The People*. It was a garish sight. But, to all newspaper men and women, a deeply impressive one.

It spoke of left-leaning independence and it spoke in a big, loud voice. But it was at this time under the increasingly eccentric command of Robert Maxwell.

Steve Lynas sat behind his desk and asked me what I wanted. 'A job,' I told him. 'But to start with, two weeks of shifts to show you what I can do.'

'Well, you seem pretty confident in your abilities, if nothing else. And I do have an empty newsroom with most of my staff abroad. I'll give you two weeks and, if you work out, some regular work.'

My gamble had paid off and my move from Wales to Fleet Street got off to a flying start. Encouraged by Phil Braund, the news desk number three, I scored quite a few page leads in my two-week trial and I was taken on as a regular freelance.

Just to make sure I didn't have all my eggs in one basket, I applied to the now defunct *Today* newspaper too. Within two weeks of leaving Wales, I was working flat out. From 9.30 a.m. to 5.30 p.m. at the *Daily Mirror*. Then from 6.30 p.m. to 3 a.m. on *Today*. My only day off was Saturday. But even that soon changed. Daily papers do not work on Saturdays as they have no Sunday edition. But they do have a news desk 2 p.m.–10 a.m. shift. And for a long time I did that shift too at *Today*.

It was exhausting work but, in your mid-twenties, easily manageable. And, of course, there was the financial incentive. My annual salary in 1990 went up from £16,500 on the *Western Mail* to just over £30,000. On top of this, I was also finding my own stories, which, if not suitable for the *Mirror* or *Today*, I sold to the *News of the World*.

Life had never been more fun. I bought a fast Peugeot GTi and an early car phone and saved enough cash to put a 30 per cent deposit down on my first home – a pretty 1930s semi in New Malden, Surrey, where I would raise my young family when they came along.

While at the *Daily Mirror*, I only had one encounter with Robert Maxwell. But it was memorable.

When the following day's rival newspapers dropped on the night news desk at around 11 p.m., the night news editor's first task was to ensure every mention of Robert Maxwell or any of his labyrinthine companies was cut out and sent to his penthouse flat upstairs if he was there. Or else to his home at Headington Hill Hall, Oxfordshire, or to a fax on board his luxury yacht, the *Lady Ghislaine*.

One night during the First Gulf War, this had been overlooked. I found myself on a late shift at the *Daily Mirror* when Scud missiles had been fired by Saddam on Tel Aviv and were in mid-air as the world held its collective breath, uncertain if they carried nuclear warheads. It was a moment every bit as tense as the moon landings for around half an hour. Maxwell's cuttings had been overlooked.

As the drama of the night suddenly relaxed, the night news editor disappeared to the lavatory and a couple of others went to the canteen for tea. I was momentarily alone. I sensed a presence behind me and I turned to see Maxwell standing in the middle of the newsroom floor in his pyjamas. He wore an enormous pair of blue silk pyjamas with a giant 'RM' monogram embroidered into the breast pocket. He stood there barefoot, immense at around 6ft 2in. and 22 stone. He looked apoplectic with rage and glared at me. Then he boomed in that famously terrifying forte fortissimo bass, 'Where's my fucking news editor?' (Everything was possessive with Maxwell – 'my newspaper', 'my editor'. And, if his editor asked for a bigger budget, 'My money!' or 'You've got your fucking hand in my fucking pockets again!')

Maxwell was apt to sack people in a flash and I was momentarily speechless as I tried to formulate the right sentence.

Maxwell, smelling strongly of spirits, moved to within three feet of me as I sat in my chair. 'I'm talking to you, mister! Where's my fucking news editor?! I've been ringing his fucking phone for five fucking minutes!'

My reply was simple and honest. 'I think he's on the toilet, Mr Maxwell.'

'ON THE FUCKING TOILET?!'

'Yes.'

'There's a fucking war on, I still haven't got my newspapers and my news editor is SITTING ON THE FUCKING TOILET?!'

By now, he was making it sound like a disciplinary offence to 'sit on a toilet', a toilet which he no doubt classed as *his*. And a sackable offence for me letting him do such an audacious thing. So I thought it best to concur. 'I'm afraid so, Mr Maxwell. I'm sorry about this.' I said this with such a quiet gravity that it somehow pointed up the ridiculousness of the situation. He turned on his heel and waddled off shouting something about a 'fucking circus not a fucking newspaper' and 'fucking sort this out NOW!'

As with all of Maxwell's overcooked, intoxicated personal interactions, the reason for his anger quickly vanished and his news editor lived to fight another day.

After a few months, three hours' sleep a night caught up with me. In those days, I smoked cigarettes, Piccadilly Number One, a brand you couldn't get from the office vending machine, and I left my desk at the *Mirror* to buy a packet from the tobacconist around the corner. It was raining, so I sprinted across the road to the shop. When I reached the other side, everything started spinning and I fell to the pavement. Getting back to my feet was hard and as I tried to stand up, I fell back down again. Eventually, I grabbed a lamp-post next to me to haul myself up. Passers-by looked at me and hurried by, thinking I was a drunkard. A kind young woman asked if I was OK and if I needed an ambulance. I didn't, it was simply fatigue that had caught up with me. I felt fine after a cup of strong tea with sugar. But I realised I needed to scale down my workload, or it – and perhaps I – would suffer.

I decided to research and write interesting feature articles for magazines and reduce my absurd shift pattern a little.

One evening, in a bar in Wandsworth, I overheard a chap talking about his girlfriend's amazing Scottish great-grandfather. The old gent was 101 and, remarkably, still working on his family farm. I introduced myself and, a few days later, I was given the phone number of the old farmer near Banchory.

I called him to arrange an interview and he agreed to meet me on his isolated farm the following week. One of the Sunday glossy magazines – I forget which now – commissioned me to fly up and paid me £1,000 for the astonishing tale.

David Henderson, born in June 1889, was indeed 101. He was approaching six feet tall and had a 44-inch chest. That morning, he had been up at 4 a.m. to supervise the sale of a lorryload of hay to another farmer – signing it off with his ancient fountain pen. And he was still selling Aberdeen Angus steak to Sainsbury's, as he had been doing since 1914. He'd bought the first mechanised tractor in Scotland in 1915 and produced the bill of sale to prove it, joking in his lilting Scottish brogue, 'I kept it in case I wanted ma' money back!' His memory was long and crystal clear and stretched back to driving the cattle to Aberdeen market in 1895 with his father. It was a remarkable tale peppered with old folklore and anecdotes such as how he could predict a long winter from the feeding patterns of local crows. It was a super tale and the grand old farmer was to live another eight years, dying in 1998 as Britain's oldest man, at the age of 109.

The story would make a decent payday for a freelance in 1990. After writing it, I strolled to the local pub, where, for the second time in just a few days, another remarkable story fell into my lap. It is a habit of mine that stories just seemed to come to me. I can take no great credit for this. I just seem, by luck, to be in the right place at the right time and it has happened hundreds of times to me.

It was the end of the First Gulf War and news desks were anxious to move on from accounts of fighting to stories of homecoming and victory. At the bar of the lonely Scottish inn, the landlord told me a tale of sorrow and tragedy. One of the local men was an RAF flyer and his parents had just received a telegram from the MoD saying their son was well and was returning home in a few days. His mother read the telegram with joy, then tragically collapsed and died on the spot. His father entered the room, saw his wife on the floor, read the telegram and died right there too. The couple were later found with the happy telegram beside them.

As you read these words, they will no doubt have gripped you with a whole range of emotions, from a sense of elation and triumph at the beginning, to distress at the tragedy rising to double tragedy, to a lingering sense of incredulity and sadness. It was a very powerful news story. But it was 11 p.m. and when I rang the *Mirror* night news desk, they calculated it was too good to simply waste in the last edition. They wanted to hold it until the following day and use it big in all editions.

By 11.30 p.m., however, it was clear from my enquiries that other newspapers had heard a rumour and had been trying to track the family down.

I got straight onto the *Mirror* news desk, warned them the story wouldn't hold and for them to use it right away. I also told them I was 'putting the story all round', an expression meaning they had no exclusive rights on the story. It was becoming too well known and it was an 'all-rounder' not an 'exclusive'.

The *Mirror* desk agreed so I filed to all the regional news desks and went to bed.

In the morning, I woke to see it splashed across several newspaper front pages, including *The Sun* and the *Mail*. But not the *Daily Mirror* or the *Daily Record*, its sister paper who shared Scottish copy with its London-based stablemate.

My pager bleeped at around 9 a.m. Steve Lynas wanted to speak to me. I thought he was about to give me a herogram for coming up with an off-diary exclusive and apologising for the night desk not using it.

Instead he told me I was 'the most unpopular man at the *Mirror*'. I had given them a story but failed to tell them I was putting it out as an 'all-rounder'. The result was they kept it back and were scooped by the rest of Fleet Street, and the editor, Roy Greenslade, wanted to know why. The *Daily Record*, who were scooped in Glasgow by their rival *Sun* (such battleground defeats left suppurating wounds) were demanding I went.

It was clear the junior member of the night news desk to whom I'd spoken had failed to communicate my message to the people who needed to know – the night news editor and the night editor.

I tried explaining.

'OK, who did you fucking tell, then? Who?!'

I've never been one to drop people in it and the only answer I could give was, 'Why don't you ask the night news desk?'

Result: all my shifts cancelled and I never set foot in the *Daily Mirror* again.

A few days later, *Today* announced it was making forty-plus redundancies. My pager bleeped again. The news editor, Steve McKinley, wanted to speak to me. 'Sorry, Nev, if we're sacking all the staff we can't keep on the freelances.'

My diary, which had been full for the next six months just a few days earlier, was now empty.

So I applied to the *Daily Star* and was given two weeks to prove myself.

On the last day of my fortnight, I looked back on a successful trial and the news desk said they were eager to take me on. All well and good. My last task on the Friday afternoon was to compile a list of 'Twenty interesting things you didn't know about the governor of the Bank of England, Robin Leigh-Pemberton'.

Nobody knew all that much about him, and nor did they care. But it was especially hard to find twenty 'interesting' things. However, I managed to knock out a decent list, which included the fact that the family name hadn't always been hyphenated.

A florid-faced fellow with garish braces and a loud Lancashire voice started complaining that this could be libellous. 'How can you say that? How the hell do you know that?' I walked over to his desk with my copies of *Debrett's*, *Who's Who* and *Who Was Who* and some reliable newspaper cuttings, and showed him how it had been altered over the generations.

I was never asked back in and I did not set foot in the building again!

The man was Peter Hill, the deputy editor. And on Fleet Street, there is a certain way to speak to your superiors. I didn't exactly tell him he was behaving in an ignorant fashion but I grant you, I probably looked as though I thought he was. And he most certainly didn't like an attitude like that, I was later told.

On Fleet Street tabloids, there are two ways to react to commonplace bullying, aggression or tirading by a superior. One way is to roll over and take it. My reaction was (literally) to stand up and intimidate the person with a volley of words and the occasional expletive. On one occasion I ventured to say to one notorious bully in front of the whole newsroom: 'You! In your office! Now!' And my relationship with my superior at the *News of the World*, Greg Miskiw, whom I sat beside for many years, was quite volatile. Greg never bullied. But his personality could be intimidating. And if I sensed it to be so, I would fire off a severe blast in his direction. I was always more aggressive to my superiors than I was with my own staff, with the happy result that I was never bullied. But, even more importantly, I never bullied anyone myself.

On this occasion, however, I lost.

Despite this string of bad results, I never once thought of going back to the provinces. I knew what I was poor at. I knew in what areas of life I was mediocre. But of one thing I was absolutely certain: I still hadn't met a tabloid reporter who could beat me on a story, no matter how far up the hierarchy they were. It was this sense of conviction that kept me going through this rocky patch.

Plus, I was lucky.

A few days later, the telephone rang and it was a call which was to launch my Fleet Street career.

In front of my typewriter in the pre-digital newspaper age at the Harrow Observer, *January 1987. With me is sub-editor Sinclair Short, who is issuing me with a final written warning for wearing a comedy moustache for work.*

CHAPTER 5

TO THE *TODAY* NEWSPAPER: THE MIKE SAMS CASE

THE TELEPHONE RANG early one evening in the hall and it was a call that was to alter the course of my life, fixing it for the next twenty years.

It was Alan Watkins, a daunting night news editor at *Today* with exacting standards and a fearsome attention to detail. His proposal was for me to come and work for him as a night news reporter on a permanent freelance basis, five or six nights a week. I accepted on the spot.

For the next couple of months I worked flat out, trying my best to dazzle by bringing in stories or knocking ones out right on deadline in a few minutes. I'd done all this before, of course, to no avail. But this time, luck was firmly on my side.

To get on in Fleet Street, you need an influential mentor and I was fortunate that Alan Watkins was mine.

A former *Sun* veteran, Alan was tough: 'Freelancers are like baby seals: if they aren't up to it, they should be clubbed and thrown out the door.' Most were thrown out the door. His appearance was forbidding. One of the least vain men I know, he won't mind me saying that 'cadaverous' probably best describes him. In his late forties then, but looking ten years older, his bald pate was encircled by wild, lengthy grey locks. His teeth bore the marks of a lifetime spent chain-smoking at his desk. He drank tea by the gallon every evening but ate nothing but sausage, egg and bacon. Alan is also one of the best news desk operators I have ever known.

Possessed of a fierce and keen intelligence, he had an encyclopaedic knowledge of news stories and the people who inhabited them. He also had an instant and instinctive reaction to what stories the readers wanted to read and which ones they didn't – what we call 'news sense'. And in the middle of a massive, breaking story just minutes from deadline, Alan would phone you or appear at your shoulder and give the calmest, most precise directions in the measured, understated tone of a BBC Radio 3 continuity announcer.

Alan's recommendations to editors on who to hire or fire were acted upon without question, and after just a few weeks, at the end of 1991, the editor, Martin Dunn, offered me a staff job.

The salary, £27,500, was less than I had earned as a freelance but it offered stability, a higher profile on the paper, better expenses, a pension, holidays etc. Speaking of holidays, there was a bizarre rota system that prevailed. Every third week, reporters got Saturday, Sunday, Monday and Tuesday off. And every sixth week, they got Wednesday, Thursday, Friday and Saturday off. Together with the six weeks' annual leave, this meant we got thirteen weeks holiday a year. I was also claiming £400 a week in expenses for dashing around the country. No wonder the paper closed!

But for the next two and a half years, I had the most exciting time of my career thus far. At first, I was employed as a 'fire-fighter', an industry term for a jobbing reporter sent at a moment's notice to cover the action here, there and everywhere.

As a fully-fledged member of the Fleet Street pack, I was instructed to obey 'Pack Rules'. When a big story breaks, a reporter from each paper is despatched to cover it and the pack forms, books into the same hotel and obeys Pack Rules. This means if someone gets an angle to the story which no one else has, they share it. If someone is absent from the pack momentarily and misses an important angle, one of the pack will be instructed to give that reporter 'a fill' – meaning the relevant contents of his notebook.

Pack Rules were drawn up decades ago by reporters on the road and are frowned upon by newspaper management as they rule out the possibility of their paper landing a belting exclusive.

But they were born out of necessity and self-preservation. Necessity because it is often impossible for one single reporter to cover every angle of the story. There may be three people at three separate addresses to speak to, for example. Or one person may be despatched to the scene of a murder to speak to neighbours while another hunts for relatives and another talks to police officers and employers. Others may try to track down an ex-wife or ex-husband of the victim. Another one may try to source a photograph. The information is then pooled and the following morning, the newspaper-reading public gets to read a fully rounded news story. The content is often the same and only the writing style differs. The job of the reporter on *The Guardian* or the *Telegraph* is often no different to the job of the reporter on *The Sun* or the *Daily Mirror*. And everyone cooperates with each other as colleagues. In the evenings, back at the hotel, the following day's work will be divided among each other over a lavish dinner and vast amounts of alcohol.

Obeying Pack Rules rarely if ever results in a big, revealing exclusive for the reporter, but allows them to sleep at night, safe in the knowledge that they won't be scooped by their rivals in the morning. A reporter who misses an important angle to a story that all the other papers have obtained will face a rough time from the office. He or she may survive one news-gathering catastrophe, if they are fortunate. But two will almost certainly see you fired, especially in the rough, tough, highly competitive tabloid market.

A reporter who dares to keep an exclusive angle to himself will see the coveted tag 'Exclusive' next to his byline and receive generous praise and maybe a bonus cheque from his editor. But he will risk being shunned by the pack and deliberately kept out of the loop on the next important story.

Reporters in this situation will normally try to pass off the exclusive angle as being obtained by someone back at their office and fed into the copy by the 'subs' (sub-editors, who lay out and design the pages). But the pack generally sifts out the truth.

It will come as no surprise to hear that I was one of those reporters who broke Pack Rules.

The first time I broke them involved an innocuous story about eight-year-old Prince William in June 1991.

The young prince was at Ludgrove School in Berkshire and was skylarking around on the school's putting green when he took an accidental blow to the head from a putter wielded by one of his school chums.

Blood was pouring from the wound and he was taken to the Royal Berkshire Hospital and then onto Great Ormond Street, where his mother, Princess Diana, rushed to his bedside.

Fleet Street went into a frenzy and every paper despatched a reporter to the scene to find out what happened and obtain a follow-up story. Teachers came and went from the school but had been ordered to say nothing. So the following day's papers were full of very little that was new.

Except *Today*, which ran a story headlined 'Exclusive by Neville Thurlbeck: School pal fears being thrown in the Tower'.

This had come about because all my fellow daily reporters had got bored with the 'no comment' replies coming from staff and had adjourned to a bar nearby. Meanwhile, I had decided to follow a female teacher who left on foot and had started walking down a road, ending up in a shop nearby. As she studied the newspapers on the stand, I casually remarked: 'I feel quite sorry for the little chap who hit him. He must feel terrible about all this stink.'

The woman, who had earlier replied 'no comment' to my questions, simply said: 'You're spot on there. He's terrified. He thinks he's going to be locked in the Tower!'

And so, with that innocuous remark, an extremely innocuous exclusive story was born!

But it marked how I would be treated by news desks forevermore. From now on, I was pigeonholed as the reporter who would be prepared to peel off from the pack and go solo in pursuit of an exclusive angle – another example of how reputations often turn on a sixpence in Fleet Street.

The news desk were delighted with this 'scoop'. Of course, looking back, it was a silly little story of little consequence. But to understand how important these things are in Fleet Street requires a little understanding of how the paper – and editors in particular – operate.

Every day, the news editor sits in a news conference in front of the editor and all the paper's executives. He or she has a news list of all the day's stories that the reporters are tackling. The editor dissects each story and wears his most fearsome expression to intimidate the news editor into action. With each story, there is the demand: 'Well, what do we have that is NEW?' Or, 'What do we have that is EXCLUSIVE?' If there is little of either, it will be thrown back at the news editor (sometimes quite literally) with words such as, 'This isn't a news list. It's a fucking WISH LIST!'

So when a reporter comes up with the goods on both counts, you are the news editor's best friend, as you could very well save him from a terrible kicking in conference. The result is that these little exclusive lines get talked up and talked up, and before you know it, your story is blazing out from the page and you are being given a bonus cheque.

From then on, when a major story broke, *Today* not only sent a reporter to cover, they sometimes parachuted me in to work in the background, digging up an exclusive.

It was a role I found I relished. I had enjoyed the camaraderie of the pack very much indeed. But the buzz of working alone, often without instruction, really excited me. And I realised it was what I could do best.

Just a few weeks into my new staff job, I was given the chance to prove myself on one of the biggest crime stories of the second half of the twentieth century, which had gripped the nation.

Michael Sams, a one-legged killer, had kidnapped a young estate agent called Stephanie Slater and was holding her to ransom.

The cash handover should have seen Sams arrested by one of the biggest police operations of modern times.

But, as the fog began to encircle the ransom drop-off point, an old railway bridge, Sams gave them the slip and made off with the cash.

A year earlier, he had killed a prostitute, Julie Dart, with a hammer as she tried to escape during an earlier ransom attempt. The depths of his villainy, his low cunning and guile, were so improbably wicked as to resemble a Victorian penny dreadful.

When Sams was eventually caught, it was my job to find his ex-wife, Jane Hammond, and make sure we had her all to ourselves.

The two major problems facing me were that every other newspaper in Fleet Street also wanted her story, and that they all had deeper pockets than *Today*. *The Sun* and the *News of the World* were prepared to pay £50,000, the *Mail* and *Mail on Sunday* a little less and the *Mirror* and *Sunday Mirror* around £35,000. My budget was £15,000!

But I had resolved that I would land the story for my paper. In fact, I was obsessively determined to do so. Obsessing about beating rivals to a story was, I am afraid, one of my most tedious characteristics. It would literally consume my day and my night. Everything was always totally focused on getting the story. With very little separating the skill sets of rival reporters, an edge can often be gained simply by working fast and working long.

To understand the national obsession with Sams, here is a brief background for younger readers.

Michael Sams was the most trickiest of crooks for the police to nail. He was as cunning as fox and utterly ruthless. A calculating psychopath with a high level of intelligence.

In July 1991, Sams, forty-nine, devised an extraordinary get-rich-quick kidnapping plot straight out of one of Edgar Wallace's more far-fetched thrillers.

He built a den by an old workshop by the river Trent in Newark, Nottinghamshire, to hold his hostage while he extorted a large ransom.

Then he put his plan into action, driving to the red-light district of Leeds and luring Julie Dart, an eighteen-year-old prostitute, into his car.

After driving her back to Newark at knifepoint, he stripped her, tied her to a chair and made her write a letter to her fiancé begging him to send cash for her release.

She was then forced into a small cell he had knocked together from old timber and metal sheeting. Sams left her there and went home, awaiting his pay day. But that night, his phone rang, alerting him to the fact that Julie had escaped. Sam had devised a crude but effective trigger alarm that caused his phone to ring if his prisoner managed to break out from the cell.

Julie found herself free from the cell but trapped inside the workshop when Sams burst in through the door. Panicking and unable to control her, he murdered her with a hammer. After wrapping her body in blankets, he put it in his car boot and dumped it in a field near Huntingdon. Despite the fact that she was dead, Sams continued to demand cash from the police, sending a ransom demand for £140,000 through the personal columns of a newspaper.

But Julie's body was soon discovered and Sam was forced to abandon his extortion attempts.

He'd failed. But he refused to give up and went back to the drawing board to refine his plan. In January 1992, he struck again.

Sams rang a Birmingham estate agent, calling himself Mr Southwall, and asked to view a small semi-detached house in the Great Barr district. On 22 January, estate agent Stephanie Slater, twenty-five, went to meet her latest client on her first appointment of the day. When she failed to return at lunchtime, her colleagues became worried.

At 12.22 p.m., Sams called her office, telling the receptionist, Sylvia Baker, 'Stephanie's been kidnapped. A ransom demand will be in the post tomorrow. If you contact police, she will die.'

Sams held a knife to Stephanie's throat, then bundled her into a car and drove her to the same den where he had kept Julie Dart, in Newark. This time he had built an escape-proof cell in the form of a lockable wheelie bin.

Stephanie was forced to strip naked, was pushed inside the bin and the lid was locked.

West Midlands Police received a ransom demand for £175,000, with a deadline set for 29 January, and were certain they were dealing with Julie Dart's killer.

Pay the money was paid, and Stephanie would be released unharmed. If not, she would die. A tape with Stephanie's anxious voice begging the police to help her was sent in the post.

On 28 January the phone rang at Stephanie's office and Sams

demanded to speak to her boss, Kevin Watt. Sams asked: 'Have you got the money ready?' Told that he had, Sams replied: 'You will get a call at three o'clock tomorrow' and hung up.

Police were secretly recording the call. It was going to prove a vital breakthrough.

Meanwhile, the money was obtained and when the call came the next day, Sams ordered Kevin Watt to drive to Glossop near Manchester.

It was the start of a long line of clues left by Sams that eventually led Watt with the bag of money to an old bridge over a disused railway in the Pennines, near Barnsley.

It was a dark, foggy night. Watt saw a tin tray on the bridge parapet and placed the cash on the tray. Down below, hiding in the gloom, Sams pulled a rope and the money fell to his feet. Clutching his loot, he jumped on a motorbike and escaped into the night.

Although Watt had been watched by dozens of undercover police, Sams had taken the cash and escaped under their noses. The bag with a radio tracker in it was still on top of the bridge.

Back at the makeshift prison, Sams opened the bin and told Stephanie she was going home. After blindfolding her, he drove her to the end of her street in Birmingham and freed her.

He thought he'd got away with it, but with Stephanie free to tell her harrowing story, the blaze of media publicity unnerved him. He rang her office and threatened receptionist Sylvia Baker.

This was his big mistake. The police had left their tape

recorder in place, and on 20 February, the tapes were played on *Crimewatch* on the BBC.

Sams's first wife, Susan Oake, watched the show and recognised her husband's voice. She called the police. Detectives grabbed Sams the next day and found his workshop, the wheelie bin and many other things Stephanie had been able to tell the police about in great detail.

At his trial, Sams admitted kidnapping Stephanie but denied the kidnap and murder of Julie. He finally confessed three days after receiving his conviction and sentence of life imprisonment in July 1993. As of 2015, he is still inside, one of a handful of dangerous killers who have been told they will never be released.

Just minutes after he was arrested, I jumped in my car and headed north at eye-watering speed, anxious to outflank the opposition.

My task was to track down and obtain the exclusive story of Sams's second wife, Jane Hammond, who had apparently remarried and appeared to have vanished into thin air. A wedding certificate in the old Somerset House showed Sams and Jane had married in November 1978 in the north of England. I raced up the M1 as fast as my Peugeot GTi would carry me – which I soon learned was very fast indeed!

In the days before the internet and computerised databases, newspaper reporters had to employ a variety of tactics to obtain information on people's whereabouts.

On this occasion, I made straight for the reference library

in the town where they had married and scoured the newspaper back editions for November 1978 for a marriage report. In less than ten minutes I had found it. And it very helpfully gave the name of a relative and the fact that she lived in Cleethorpes, Lincolnshire. I realised this would be the lady who could lead the Fleet Street pack to Jane, so I was keen that it didn't find its way into their hands.

To mask the sound of the page being ripped from the binder and therefore for ever lost to my colleagues in equal hot pursuit, I issued a very long, hard cough! And after fifty pairs of eyes had finished glaring at me and returned to their reading material, I stuffed the report into my jacket pocket.

As I left the building, heading towards me came two reporters who had been detailed by the pack to do the very same work I had just completed. There was Kevin Ludden from *The Sun* – a tenacious ferret of a newsman with a facial appearance that seemed to encourage that view. Even more ominous, he was with Harry Cooke from the *Daily Express*. I realised I was up against some very tough opposition. Harry (sadly no longer with us) had a fearsome reputation and had been a Fleet Street heavyweight since the early 1970s. Working alone, I didn't want to be spotted or the pack would go out of their way to keep tabs on me and neutralise my solo efforts. So I darted into a tobacconist and watched as they strolled by and into the library on their fruitless quest.

Working alone is not without its risks. If the pack found Jane first, I would have been cut out of the deal as I hadn't cooperated in the pack hunt. My newspaper would have been the only one not to carry her story and my name would have been mud. In fact, at such an early stage in my career, it could have dealt my reputation a terminal blow.

Looking back, I wonder why I risked everything by going out on a limb so boldly and so early in my career. But at the time I don't think I gave it a second thought, such is the arrogance and confidence of youth. As Ludden and Cooke searched in vain for the wedding report, I sped off for Cleethorpes to track down Jane's relative, with my speedometer and rev counter competing for pole position.

Cleethorpes is a Lincolnshire seaside resort of 31,000 souls. Jane's relative wasn't in the telephone directory so finding her in those pre-internet days was a slow, laborious process. Today, a reporter will use Facebook, Twitter and Google to locate their target in minutes. In 1992, it meant going to the council, asking for the electoral register and speed-reading hundreds of pages of names and addresses.

By the time I arrived at 6 p.m., the council offices were closed and I was facing a frustrating fifteen-hour wait until they reopened at 9 a.m. the following day. I was keenly aware that the pack would eventually catch up with me and the advantage I had secured would dissolve in a mass scrum on her doorstep, where my voice would be just one of many competing for Jane's relative's help.

Tracking down people late at night when the electoral roll was locked in a council cupboard involved a lot of footslogging, knocking on doors, street after street, until it became disrespectfully late – anywhere between 9.30 p.m. and 11 p.m., depending on the time of year and the seriousness of the story. But I had discovered quite early in my career that an advantage could be gained over those choosing this highly pedestrian approach.

In the late '80s and early '90s, it was the habit of millions to rent films on videos. A small town such as Cleethorpes would have a couple of dozen late-night shops with a small video library where one could rent a film for a small fee. But, crucially, in order to rent, you had to register your name and address.

These small shop owners were normally cheerful, helpful Gujarati Asians who had been kicked out of Uganda by Idi Amin. A telephone call would always elicit suspicion. But a personal visit, the purchase of a packet of cigarettes and a polite enquiry as to the whereabouts of Mr or Mrs So-and-so normally worked. I never referred directly to the 'video hire directory', as this would appear too professionally inquisitive and lead to a barrage of questions. But a simple 'I'm trying to get a message to Mr So-and-so, who may be a customer of yours and I wonder if you could help me please' always, always worked.

There is a misapprehension among the general public, and even among certain journalists themselves, that it takes aggression to win on a story and it is the noisy, blustering, foot-in-the-door merchant who breaks the scoops. The truth is quite the opposite. It is often quiet, polite persistence that wins the day. 'Persuading' people to part with information is far harder than 'asking for someone's assistance'. Human beings enjoy giving something to someone by way of help. And if that happens to be information, so much the better for a journalist. But try to extract that information by hectoring or slyness and you will usually end up with the door in your face.

Armed with a hotel copy of the Yellow Pages, I set about visiting all the video shops in Cleethorpes in search of Jane Hammond's relative.

Within the hour, I was on her doorstep.

When you are in search of the in-laws of a brutal killer, you have certain preconceptions of what they may be like. The Hammonds did not meet any of them. They were a very respectable, decent, hard-working family. But Jane's relative was unsure if she wanted to help. She explained that Jane was abroad on holiday with her husband and wouldn't be back for a week. When she returned, she would pass on a message, she said. But she wouldn't interrupt their holiday.

With the rest of the pack perhaps just a few hours behind me, this delay would be fatal. I asked her to reconsider. She suggested I called back after work the following day, a full eighteen hours later. Sufficient time for the pack to steal back my advantage and take over en masse.

I had no choice but to agree. We arranged to meet at her house at 5 p.m. I got there at noon. And then, as I had predicted, by 3 p.m. the pack arrived. Cooke from the *Express* and Ludden from *The Sun* were there together with assorted colleagues from the *Mail*, *Star*, *Mirror*, *News of the World*, *Sunday Mirror* and *Sunday People*, as well as a host of news agencies, including PA.

Now that PA was trumpeting to the world about the relative, even TV cameras started turning up. Then the *Telegraph* and *The Times*. In fact, the only ones missing were *The Independent* and *The Guardian*. I'd lost my advantage.

Jane's relative was mortified. Stunned and frightened by the unexpected deluge of reporters and cameras, she asked us all to go away and come back in the morning. The pack all moved off to the same hotel to roister in the bar, with Pack Rules all nicely in place to ensure everyone moved and swooped together in perfect formation like a flock of starlings practising for their winter migration. A reporter was nominated to remain quietly outside and watch in case they did a midnight flit.

Back in the hotel room, I considered every option available to regain my advantage. In the end, I came up with something so cavalier it would either work spectacularly or blow up in my face and see me ostracised by the pack.

I packed my bag and quietly checked out of the hotel at midnight when the roistering had finished and the pack's nightwatchman would hopefully have left the scene.

As I turned the corner into the relative's road, I could see the watchman's car had gone. The downstairs lights were on, indicating the family hadn't gone to bed. I knocked on the door. Jane's relative had been joined by her brother, a kindly, level-headed fellow. I explained the situation. The pack would be back in the morning and the house would be besieged for the foreseeable future. My solution, if they would care to take it, would be to pack their bags straight away, get in my car, and I would put them up in a good hotel until it had all blown over. All I required from them was to pass on a message to Jane when she returned and hopefully effect an introduction. Nothing more.

At 12.30 a.m., we all sped off into the night.

CHAPTER 6

FLEET STREET FUGITIVE

AS WE HEADED off to destination unknown, I rang Alan Watkins on the night desk from my early, primitive car phone to deliver news of our sudden breakthrough.

Alan was emotionally taciturn and never one to display excitement. On this occasion, he didn't say anything at all. Nothing. I thought the line was dead, so I hung up and rang again. 'Fuck me, young thing!' (I was always 'young thing' to Watkins if I was in his good books. The rest of the time, 'young Thurlbeck'.) He had heard but was speechless, he confessed. Then he clicked straight into news desk overdrive. 'Get everyone into an out-of-the-way hotel. Book in under false names. Make sure no one finds out where you are.'

Jane Hammond was on holiday abroad for a week so I had to tread water waiting for her return, keeping her relative out of the reach of the pack and the inevitable monstering that would ensue if they found her.

The morning after our midnight flit, my car phone, which had remained switched on overnight, had registered thirty-four missed calls. My pager also received more than a dozen messages from reporters who had returned to the Hammond house to find no one there and me missing too. Most were along the lines of, 'Hi, mate. Where are you?' Some were a little more blunt.

A few days later, Jane returned and I signed her exclusively to *Today* for £15,000. By this time, the pack had got wind of her address and were waiting for her return home. So to avoid a scrum of competing chequebooks during which we would inevitably be outbid, I got a message to her via her relative to meet at an isolated hotel.

I chose the Lodore Swiss in Borrowdale in the Lake District. It had been my venue for several special celebrations and romantic assignations in the late 1970s and was the perfect hideout for the interview and photoshoot.

Jane was (and I presume still is) an elegant, intelligent woman. She'd met Sams on the rebound and quickly came to regret it.

She was forty-six at the time of the interview and told of her life of hell while married to the brutal killer. When she had left him, he turned up at her father's funeral to find her. Terrified that he would turn up, grieving Jane had stayed away. Furious Sams told her mother he would hunt her down and kill her with a shotgun. The pair had married in 1978 and separated at the end of 1980. But the scars still remained.

On 8 July 1993, Sams was jailed for the rest of his life for
Julie Dart's murder and the kidnapping of Stephanie Slater.
That evening, we put together our story on the background
to one of the most sensational crime stories of modern times,
with the front-page headline 'Kidnapper, Killer, Crazy Man.
My Life with Michael Sams'. The story was scheduled to run
on pages 1, 2, 3, 4, 5, 6, 7, 8 and a two-page centre spread.

For a little paper with barely 450,000 readers, we had out-
flanked and outgunned the combined efforts of the rest of
Fleet Street.

But there was significant postscript to this cloak-and-dag-
ger episode. The *News of the World* had a belter of a story up
its sleeve for the coming Sunday. They had signed up Sams's
best man, Carl Metcalfe. The reporter on the buy-up was the
then deputy news editor Greg Miskiw. And the fee they had
promised Metcalfe was £50,000. The pack had discovered this
and there was fevered speculation that his story must have
been dynamite to command such a price.

So I had decided to try to find out for myself. As well as
my *Today* photo-pass, I also still carried my old, more neutral,
News International one from my freelance days. Armed with
this, I drove the 250 miles to Metcalfe's Yorkshire home and
knocked on the door. I told him my name and that I worked
for News International. I told him I was a colleague of Greg
Miskiw (true, as we both worked for NI titles). I then told him
I needed him to go over his interview again with me as Greg
has mislaid it and would be in deep trouble with the editor.

He did, and he revealed an extraordinary tale about how Sams had tried to rope him into kidnapping a wealthy industrialist's daughter some years earlier. And how, when he visited him on remand, Sams had boasted of the Julie Dart murder while denying it to police.

We had pinched the *News of the World* splash from right under their noses. They were furious and made it known within the company that they were absolutely livid. But, to their credit, they would invite me to take a staff job with them soon after.

The editor, the late Richard Stott, was delighted, and sent me on a ten-day, all-expenses-paid cruise around the Mediterranean.

Ten years later, as I sat next to Miskiw as his deputy in the investigations unit and later on the news desk as his deputy news editor, I used to remind my boss (and friend) how I had scooped him so dramatically all those years earlier – usually for the benefit of junior reporters, who would chortle along as I chided him.

Greg's reaction was always the same. His face would redden and he would utter a voluble volley of expletives which would last about thirty seconds. It was like pressing the bass pedal of an organ: just one touch and a thunderous boom would come out. If Greg was ever being unfair to a reporter, which to his credit was very rare, I used to whisper to the reporter, 'Watch what happens when I remind him of this,' and then tell the story again and watch him explode over an event that had taken place ten years earlier.

Such is the rivalry and the gladiatorial nature of Fleet Street reporting.

Looking a little sceptical. Caught mid-interview, June 1987.

CHAPTER 7

A ROW WITH GORDON BROWN, AN UNDERCOVER CATASTROPHE AND MEETING ROSE WEST

*T*ODAY WAS A mid-market tabloid when I first started working there in 1990. A more colourful, optimistic version of the *Daily Mail* but without the attitude – or the readers.

It pioneered colour printing and was very female-friendly when Eddy Shah launched it in 1986. Its future looked promising when Rupert Murdoch's News International bought it from its second owner, Tiny Rowland's Lonrho.

Readership levels fluctuated but peaked at around 600,000. It seemed to attract the middle-class reader who was irritated by what they perceived to be the *Mail*'s Blimpish, gloomy analysis of British society, and by the frivolity of the *Mirror* and *The Sun*.

The newsroom was staffed with superb reporters. Anne Robinson was a columnist. Tina Weaver, a future *Sunday Mirror* editor, sat next to me. Opposite me, when he wasn't in the House of Commons, sat Alastair Campbell. It often amuses me to hear people who don't know Alastair describing him in unsavoury terms. Their knowledge of him is gleaned only from cowed politicians who describe him as 'bullying', 'controlling' or 'an attack dog'. I only ever found him affable, engaging and witty, although more than a little pugilistic (at the *Mirror*, he once famously chinned a reporter for making fun of his boss Robert Maxwell's demise).

As Tony Blair's director of communications, he had one of the toughest briefs in the history of PR – to ensure the serried ranks of Fleet Street didn't bomb a Labour government to smithereens, as had been its habit over the previous thirty years. It was one man against many. And he won. He recognised that 'affable Alastair' wasn't going to be the best person to put into battle. Enter 'Attack-Dog Alastair'. He was armed with a brilliant mind and a shrewd understanding of how Fleet Street, Westminster and the electorate engaged on various platforms. He was a brilliant political editor at *Today* and the *Daily Mirror* and arguably one of the greatest communicators and political strategists of the 1990s.

Another veteran political editor, Eben Black, was with us, eventually doing the rounds of virtually the entire News International stable, occupying senior roles with distinction at *The Sun*, the *News of the World* and the *Sunday Times*. We forged a friendship on the road and we remain the very best of chums to this day. Cheryl Stonehouse went on to the *Mail* along with Nick Craven and Christian Gysin, Olga Craig to the *Telegraph*. Jon Craig became political editor for Sky News. The veteran royal editor Charlie Rae dominated the newsroom with his larger-than-life frame and personality as he had done on *The Sun* earlier and would do again later.

It was an incredibly cohesive office with enormous *esprit de corps*, which spilled over into the bar every night after work. I rarely attended these champagne-fuelled events in the Wapping bars, partly because I had a young family whom I was desperate to see in the evening, but also because I have never socialised much with work colleagues. Not because I didn't care for their company but because I can be notoriously unsociable, even to the point of refusing to attend the annual *News of the World* Christmas party. I have rarely attended parties of any sort since my student days. And the thought of corporate Christmas parties, corporate Christmas cards and a corporate speech from an editor makes me shudder. On *Today*, my colleagues chose to interpret my lack of socialising as meanness and used to make amusing jokes out of it at my expense. In truth, I think it simply boils down to the fact that, no matter how much I love my job, I never liked talking shop. My family are all great talkers but after work in the evening, it was never about the job. And when we have people round for lunch or dinner, I always arrange with my wife to steer the conversation away from work matters when it inevitably crops up.

I've always jollied along well with colleagues in the office and rarely made an enemy. But, in truth, I was still a bit of an outsider by choice and remained so for the rest of my career, much the same as I was at school. And with increasing amounts of time spent alone, on the road, digging away behind the scenes, my 'outsider' status grew over the years.

Landing the Michael Sams scoop made me temporarily unpopular among certain opposition colleagues, including those at the *News of the World*. But, in time, this morphed into a good-natured cat-and-mouse game when I was spotted on the road by the pack. When chasing stories on the road, I would assiduously avoid fellow reporters, making sure I booked into a hotel off the beaten track and always under a false name. And if someone had to be interviewed, I'd be on the doorstep at 7 a.m. – considered 'indecently early' even by news desks. This way, I not only avoided bumping into the pack, I also frequently managed to get to the target as they were getting into their car at 7.30 a.m. for a long commute. Fleet Street has long considered 8.30 a.m. to be about the most respectable time to knock on someone's door. But these days, most people have long departed. By the time they returned to face the pack at 7 or 8 p.m., it was too late for first editions. Although we were always guided to knock after 8.30 a.m., I was never once criticised for people ringing up to complain that I'd got them out of bed at 7.30 a.m.!

Being in the good books of Richard Stott certainly saved me from the sack after I engaged in a particularly fierce verbal exchange with Gordon Brown in 1994, when he was shadow Chancellor of the Exchequer.

Bank interest rates were then decided and set by the government of the day, before the incoming Labour government of 1997 put the Bank of England in control of the task. The incumbent Tory government had increased the rate and, in the office one Sunday, I was asked to get a reaction from Brown for the Monday morning edition. I had recently purloined the excellent BBC political contacts book, which had the numbers of every politician in the country, and I tracked down Brown to his Scottish constituency home. Would he care to give his view and that of the Labour Party on the government's interest rate hike a couple of days earlier? I am afraid his response made me see red.

'How dare you call me when I am having Sunday lunch? Don't you realise there are much more junior members of my staff on call to deal with silly questions from *Today* reporters?'

My reply, I am afraid, was blunt. 'What makes you think you're so fucking special that you can't spend two minutes telling the electorate what your party thinks of the new interest rate?'

Brown fired off a tirade of outrage, hectoring me and warning me that he knew Richard Stott and he would be having words. That only made me madder. 'Go fuck yourself.' He was still spitting feathers when I hung up on him, got up from my chair and walked straight into Stott's office. I told his secretary it was urgent and that the shadow Chancellor was about to call him and I needed to brief him.

Stotty was a tough editor and a Labour man through and through. He had twice edited both the *Daily Mirror* and *The People*. He was a stout, muscular man with a thick neck, a barking voice and a reddish complexion that lent him the perpetual air of a man about to be consumed by an apoplectic rage.

'What's up, Nev?'

I told him. Stotty looked at me across his desk, his face deadpan. 'I see, I see, and what did you say?'

'I'm afraid I told him to go and fuck himself.'

Stotty paused for a few moments as he weighed up all the options against the admission I had just made. Fire me? Suspend me? Then he announced his decision. 'I see. Well, if he calls me, I'll tell him to go and fuck himself as well!' Brown never called.

Years later, we used to share early morning swims in an outdoor swimming pool, even in the depths of winter, with Stotty blowing like a whale as he went an even brighter shade of red in the sub-zero temperatures. One morning, I reminded him of the Brown episode and he guffawed. 'Well, I admired your guts for standing up to the bugger. And I admired your guts for holding your hands up straight away and telling me. How could I fire you?'

The episode said a lot about both of us I think. Stotty was a fierce but very fair man. And when I make a mistake (I've made many), I try to hold my hands up straight away.

Richard Stott died from pancreatic cancer in July 2007, aged sixty-three.

*T*oday was a great little daily newspaper. And it wasn't afraid to go the extra mile and throw time and money at a serious investigation.

One rumour doing the rounds in the House of Commons in the early 1990s concerned a government minister and his preference for rent boys. We'd heard the *News of the World* had investigated the tip but had given up. *Today* decided they would have a look, and put me on the case. I was detailed to follow the minister around and watch for any suspicious meetings.

Following a government minister isn't easy and no training is given for this aspect of the job. In fact, no training is given for any aspect of the job. You are meant to arrive on Fleet Street fully formed and conversant with every part of it. In reality, no one is. And you have to find your way along as you go and hope your mistakes don't come to anyone's attention.

Ministers have chauffeurs and are surrounded by staff and sometimes security. So the chances of being rumbled are pretty high. After a few days, you will inevitably be noticed. If you are still on his tail after a week, story or no story, your undercover skills will at least be appreciated by your news desk.

This particular minister was my first political quarry. And

through some minor miracle, I had managed to remain on his tail, unobserved, for five weeks. I took a room in a hotel in his constituency, followed him to local restaurants and to those in town. I followed him to the Commons, placing a motorbike in the vicinity to alert me when he left so I could pick him up. The same when he went into Downing Street.

There was no sign of any rent boys and the rumour, so prevalent on Fleet Street in 1992, has long been given as an example of an apocryphal story with absolutely no basis in fact.

But *Today* wanted me to persist. And so I carried on. Driving two cars behind him so as not to stand out; sitting at the other end of a restaurant; walking on the opposite side of the street; hat on, hat off; jacket on, jacket off. I was employing all the usual comedy/mystery undercover techniques bar hiding behind a copy of the *Daily Telegraph* with eyeholes cut out.

But my undercover rigmarole seemed surprisingly effective. However, one evening when he sauntered into a pizzeria for a light supper, disaster struck from a clear blue sky.

Parking myself as usual at the opposite end of the restaurant, I ordered a pizza and some chillies and made sure I had enough cash to plonk down on the table should I need to leave at the double.

Another surprising aspect to undercover surveillance is the imperative to try to relieve oneself when a safe moment presents itself. With the minister seated at his table, this seemed like a perfectly safe moment to do so. And after rubbing the chillies onto my pizza, I left my table to visit the gents.

Two minutes later, I was back at my table to see the minister's first course arrive.

Two minutes is also the length of time it takes for chilli to start scorching the male member and elicit shouts of alarm and distress.

Alarmed and distressed, I gyrated in my seat. And shouted.

The pain was severe. I tried deep breaths, then sharp intakes of breath. The pain got worse. I broke into a sweat. People had started looking at me, so I got up from my seat and made for the front door, stooping as I clutched my groin and scuttled gingerly in mincing little footsteps outside.

The minister hadn't noticed and I clutched a lamp-post, waiting for the pain to subside.

Seconds later, I was followed by a waitress who thought I was having a heart attack and insisted on calling an ambulance. Eager to avoid further compromising the undercover operation – to say nothing of the mounting embarrassment – I levelled with her. 'No. Please, I just forgot to wash my hands before going to the gents! I've got chilli on my willy.'

Almost as embarrassed as me, she walked back into the restaurant as I regained my composure. Five minutes later I re-entered, wearing what I hoped would be my best nonchalant expression.

Every member of staff burst into laughter. They had clearly been well briefed by their chortling colleague who had attempted my rescue. But the laughter didn't subside, it grew louder. Like actors corpsing on stage, the nervous appreciation that they shouldn't be laughing at me just poured petrol onto their laughter, which had now become something approaching a roar. One fellow attempted to stifle a raucous, full-blown belly laugh. Much to my dismay, he failed.

By now, everyone in the restaurant was looking at me. The minister even stood up to get a better view.

Never has a journalist's cover been broken more spectacularly or embarrassingly.

Disconcertingly, despite not having a shred of evidence, the news desk wanted me to front up the minister and put the allegations to him. I tackled him on his front doorstep as he arrived by chauffeur-driven car. His face turned white, his fists clenched and he walked towards me as if to strike me. His chauffeur put down the red despatch boxes he was carrying and stepped in between us to keep us apart. If it wasn't for this intervention, I'm convinced he would have punched me. And quite frankly, I wouldn't have blamed him.

A happy adjunct to this heroic failure was the accidental conception of my daughter in the nearby hotel, prompting a hasty wedding and a long and happy marriage!

Long stakeouts are the norm when you are undercover and trying to break the story everyone else wants. Sometimes, as in this case, they can be frustratingly fruitless. Returning to base empty handed after five weeks of work made me feel sheepish and eager to prove myself all over again. It also meant five weeks had gone by without a single byline in the paper.

If a reporter goes on a second mission that ends in failure, it can mysteriously trigger another and then another, failure breeding insecurity breeding even more failure. And a long barren patch can prove fatal to a young journalist's career on the tabloids. I became extremely driven, spending sometimes up to nine months a year away from home and on the road, leaving my wife at home to bear the brunt of bringing up a young daughter, followed soon after by another. So my determination to keep ahead of the game came at a cost as I missed an awful lot of their formative years. But it meant the homecoming was ever more joyful. For the purposes of this book, I will refer to my daughters by the childhood nicknames I gave them as babes in arms and which the family still use to this day: 'Boo' is my eldest and 'Bee' my youngest. They are my greatest achievements and the source of my greatest pride.

In March 1994, it looked like another long, fruitless undercover job was about to begin. I was in the Swiss ski resort of Zermatt tracking down one of Princess Diana's several lovers (I forget which one now), when the office suddenly called me back. They wanted me to track down Rosemary West, who was in a police safe house somewhere in Gloucestershire.

Her husband, Fred West, was in police custody being questioned on multiple murders as body after body was being dug up at their home at 25 Cromwell Street, Gloucester. Rose was being kept at a police safe house out of the media glare. On my return, it became clear to me from several police sources that Rose West was being strung along. The police, quite naturally, wanted her to give them as much information as possible about the sickening activities that had taken place behind closed doors. The police safe house was just a ruse to make her believe the police were treating her as a victim rather than a suspect.

Lodgers, babysitters and children, including the couple's eldest daughter Heather, aged sixteen, as well as complete strangers, had been picked up off the street and were tortured, abused and killed before being buried in the cellar or under the patio of their house.

Some were subjected to lingering deaths. Breathing tubes were pushed through mummy-style masks made of yards of packing tape to keep them alive as sexual playthings until their usefulness was over.

As long as the police pretended they regarded her as a potential victim of Fred West's murderous tyranny, there was the possibility Rose would start providing vital evidence incriminating her husband. Then, when she stopped talking, on would go the handcuffs. My mission was to track down and get a photograph of the woman we believed would very soon be revealed as one of Britain's most notorious mass murderers.

I kept in close contact with several sources, one of whom narrowed down my search considerably by revealing that Rose West was being kept in a safe house in the Gloucestershire market town of Dursley. With 5,800 souls, this was still a needle-in-a-haystack job. The office thought so too and called me back. Then, when walking down Kingshill Road, I noticed a Kwik Save store, a discount supermarket chain once favoured by those on low incomes. This was the very place where Rose West would do her grocery shopping, I figured.

I held on in Dursley and kept the shop under a close watch for three days. Nothing. Then, on the fourth day, a woman in glasses and with a rounded figure shuffled towards the main door and into the shop. She looked a little like Rose West. But not convincingly so. I needed to get a close look and followed her up the frozen food aisle as she threw peas and sweetcorn into her trolley and I threw peas and sweetcorn into mine.

I had asked the photographer working with me to remain outside and take a picture of her as she left. But still, I couldn't be confident it was Rose West. We needed to be more than confident, too. We needed to be absolutely certain. If we printed a picture of the local librarian and branded her Rose West, heads would roll. So I kept on following this middle-aged woman with the matronly figure as she casually picked her way around the shelves. She turned to look at me and saw me briefly staring at her but betrayed no trace of anxiety. This, to me, was a bad sign. I had assumed she would have been intensely nervous of being spotted by the press ... unless she was simply super-confident her secret hideaway was secure. I optimistically hoped it was the latter and followed her to the checkout. With her goods packed into carrier bags, she opened her purse and pulled out a credit card. I had a split second to try to read the name on it before she handed it to the cashier.

And a split second to decide how to read it without ringing alarm bells. With one swift movement I stood right next to the woman, bent over the conveyor belt to look right at the card and said to the cashier, 'Ah good! You take credit cards here. I didn't think you did.'

The name on the credit card was that of Rosemary West. I stood back from my role as a journalist and viewed her as any human being would. Except, through my sources, I knew she was heavily implicated in the brutal murders of at least ten girls and young women. I looked at her face. It wasn't an evil face. It was the face of a frumpy, working-class woman from the sticks, nothing more. I often think you can tell an unpleasant person when they get to middle age, as lines begin to form in the wrong places. But not Rose West. She was very hirsute, with dozens of black whiskers trailing from her upper lip and chin, something the photographs never seem to pick up. And I got close enough to discover she had an appalling personal hygiene problem – again, something I haven't read about anywhere. But these things of course don't amount to tangible signs of evil and I was totally wrong-footed by the banality of her appearance, demeanour and mannerisms.

Outside the store, I began questioning her about the murders as the photographer began taking his pictures, scurrying backwards as Rose West scurried forwards while she made her way, saying nothing, towards her safe house. We broke the story the next day.

Gloucestershire Constabulary's Cromwell Street Enquiry

dryly notes: 'On 25 March 1994 Mrs West was living at Dursley when she was photographed by the media. It was then necessary at very short notice to remove her to other police accommodation at Cheltenham, where she remained until 25 April 1994 when she was arrested.'

Rose West was jailed for life in 1995 for the brutal, sadistic murders of ten women and girls and is probably one of the most evil individuals we will know in our lifetimes.

But, stripped of her position of power and control, Rose West's banality reigned. It was much the same with Adolf Eichmann in 1961, when, shorn of his uniform of death, and the instruments and levers of demented power long confiscated, he sat in the dock like a meek filing clerk, to the astonishment of the world.

The political theorist Hannah Arendt described this incongruous phenomenon in her 1963 work *Eichmann in Jerusalem: A Report on the Banality of Evil*. She argues that the great evils of the Holocaust were not perpetrated by fanatics or psychopaths but by ordinary people who accepted the rules of their state and therefore participated with the view that their actions were normal.

In Rose West's case, Fred West made the rules and his subservient acolyte followed them blindly, hurling her victims into oblivion. But on 25 March 1994, before I had seen the name on her credit card, I would have trusted her to mind my daughter's pram.

A few weeks later, however, I was to be confronted with the

most unambiguous vision of evil, so stark and Miltonic in its hellishness that, nearly twenty years later, I still don't think I have fully recovered from it.

CHAPTER 8

THE LOUGHINISLAND MASSACRE

O N 18 JUNE 1994, I was driving back to my hotel from a restaurant on the outskirts of Belfast when I made a telephone call that propelled me into the blackest day of my career.

I had been despatched to cover an incident in which a crazed young man had stormed his old school with a home-made flamethrower and run amok in an examination hall, badly burning some of the students. At around 10.30 p.m., I pulled up to make a phone call to the Royal Ulster Constabulary press office to find out if the perpetrator had been charged so I could update the story I had filed earlier.

The press officer updated me, then added, 'We've just had reports coming in of a major incident in Loughinisland so you may want to keep in touch with us when it becomes clearer.'

Alarm bells rang immediately. For the RUC, in its long, battle-weary experience of bloodshed and violence, to describe an incident as 'major' was significant. I looked at the map and saw that Loughinisland, a small village 21 miles south of Belfast, was just a couple of miles away.

I arrived with the smell of gunfire still in the air. Ambulances and paramedics rushed around the tiny village pub, The Heights. Several villagers stood rooted to the spot, like statues.

In the panic and confusion, no one stopped me as I walked out of the dark towards the pub's front door. I wished they had. A loose pyramid of bodies lay inside the bar. Slumped forwards and all shot in the back. At the end of the humble snug and at the foot of the counter, another man lay dead. Shot in the back as he tried to make a getaway towards the gents' lavatory. The area smelled very much like a butcher's shop and I reeled back.

About half an hour earlier, the rural village pub had been a jolly mix of locals, all sitting down to watch the World Cup game between Italy and Jack Charlton's Ireland – 'Jack's lads', as they were fondly called. It would have been a wonderful, carnival atmosphere in the bar that night.

Instead, at 10.10 p.m., two members of the loyalist Ulster Volunteer Force (UVF) wearing boiler suits and balaclavas walked in carrying assault rifles. The happy band of neighbours had their backs to them as they watched the TV and cheered on 'Jack's lads'. They didn't stand a chance.

Witnesses later reported that the gunmen ran off laughing and sped off in their getaway car, a red Triumph Acclaim, leaving six men dead and five injured. It remains one of the worst atrocities ever committed in Britain. They have never been caught.

The attack was a reprisal in the tit-for-tat killings that blighted the Irish nation at the time. This time, Catholics were the victims.

The dead were Barney Greene, eighty-seven, Adrian Rogan, thirty-four, Malcolm Jenkinson, fifty-three, Daniel McCreanor, fifty-nine, Patrick O'Hare, thirty-five, and Eamon Byrne, thirty-nine.

At eighty-seven, Mr Greene was one of the oldest victims of the Troubles. Mr McCreanor used to take him to the same pub every Saturday night for fellowship and companionship. For the occasion, Mr Greene, with his old-style working-class pride, would put on his best brown boots and polish them to a brilliant shine, don his felt trilby and they would saunter off together – that evening for the final time.

The following day, the village was full of journalists from every part of the world. Hundreds of them, representing news organisations from every continent, flown in from their country of origin or their European outposts. By now, the crime scene had been properly cordoned off and the police were in full control when they gave their first press conference. Considering the tragic nature of the killings, it was an astonishingly anodyne affair. 'We are looking for two males, driving a red vehicle, registration number...' And so on and so forth. And no mention that these people had been shot in the back in an act of sickening cowardice.

The press corps all went back to the Europa Hotel in Belfast to write and file their copy.

I went back to write mine too. But armed with a world-exclusive scoop. I would be the only journalist to report and highlight the depths of brutality and cowardice the Troubles had sunk to. It was decided with the news desk that I should heavily sanitise the copy but weave in the very emotive fact that they were all shot in the back.

I had my scoop. But I felt very uneasy. As so often in my career, I was simply in the right place at the right time, like a lucky centre forward. I could hardly take credit for it. And how could I grandstand on the back of six dead men? I thought long and hard about it. For the first and only time in my career, I shared my information with my colleagues. I invited about twenty reporters from various organisations to my room, where I fully briefed them in total silence. Everyone then left and let the world know how low the Troubles had sunk.

I've never regretted my decision. As a reporter, I was in the right place at the right time. But as a human being, I was in the wrong place at the wrong time.

No scoop. No matter. 18 June 1994 was not about me. It was about others.

Back in England, I struggled for a while with the images and what they signified. I was living in New Malden, Surrey, but I was still close to the vicar of my previous church, St Luke's, in Wimbledon Park, the Rev. David Wiles.

David made one of his occasional visits to our new home

and helped me enormously with my emotions and my crisis in faith, for which I will always be in his debt. He asked me to address the matter to the congregation but I realised I wouldn't be able to hold it together.

I still feel bonded to these six men through a shared moment of deep, personal intimacy. I very much hope they are resting peacefully. And I hope their loved ones are able to smile again.

I make no political comment here. But to those who would fight in Ulster and Ireland, please remember Barney Greene as I do: his spectacles askew on his face, his hat knocked off his head, his brown boots shining proudly in that sudden silence.

God bless them all.

CHAPTER 9

TO THE *NEWS OF THE WORLD*: COLIN STAGG AND THE RACHEL NICKELL MURDER

IN JUNE 1994, Patsy Chapman, the *News of the World* editor who had banished me, believing me a spy for the *Sunday Mirror*, finally stepped down from the paper. The following day, my phone rang at my *Today* desk. It was Alex Marunchak, the *News of the World* news editor. 'Hi, it's Alex. She's gone. Do you want to come back?'

Alex was one of the most respected news editors on Fleet Street and part of a legendary Ukrainian double act with Greg Miskiw, his deputy. He was the master of subterfuge and had orchestrated the exposure of errant politicians and pop stars on the paper for over a decade. Now in his early forties, with silver hair and a matching moustache which he stroked down one side when pensive, he had the most inscrutable face I had ever seen.

Poaching staff from stablemate papers was looked upon very badly by News International, unless the member of staff had made the move first. Alex set up a meeting designed to encourage me to do just that. In typical Marunchak style, he suggested a meeting in an obscure, quiet part of the Wapping HQ, bumping into each other in a lift 'by accident' so we could continue talking as we walked on our way.

For four years, I had been doing a job on *Today* that would fit well on the *News of the World* – working alone and behind the scenes. But I was extraordinarily happy on *Today*, a fact I impressed upon him: firstly because it was true, and secondly because I wanted to find out what his salary bottom line was. Appear too keen and I'd be fobbed off with just a couple of thousand pounds more. 'What's your salary now?' he enquired. '£32,000,' I replied, inflating it by £3,000 more than the actual amount. 'That's no problem, we'll give you £36,000,' he added. This would normally clinch a deal. £7,000 more on my salary was an awful lot of money in 1994. But I was determined to hold out for more, even if it meant losing the job. I said I'd think about it.

The following day, I rang him and said I'd only come for £40,000 as I was really very content at *Today*, given lots of autonomy, and you couldn't put a price on all that. Alex agreed and I joined the paper in August, starting the biggest adventure of my newspaper career.

Coming back to the *News of the World* felt like the most natural thing in the world. If I'm honest, it's where I really belonged. And my first day felt like a homecoming too. There was Clive Goodman again, offering to buy me a cup of tea and cackling his rasping chain smoker's laugh at the 'Thurlbeck Spy Scandal', which had done for me five years earlier. Bob Warren, who had moved into an executive editor's role by now, came over to say, 'Nice to have you back.' Having Bob's seal of approval meant a lot to me. Piers Morgan, the new editor, then aged twenty-eight, bounded over and shook my hand, adding, 'We've heard great things about you.' I felt totally welcome. But that did little to ease the sense of apprehension I had inside.

I had suddenly gone from a junior reporter on the smallest paper on Fleet Street to a senior reporter on the biggest newspaper in the English-speaking world.

There was no room for novices at the *News of the World*. There was no such thing as a training programme for anything. If you had to pose as a paedophile to expose a child sex ring, or as a gun-runner or as a hit man, you would be expected to be able to do it.

Sooner or later, you are singled out for a particular discipline on Sunday newspapers, although not necessarily exclusively confined to it. Reporters will follow their natural inclinations when building contacts and will favour meeting people from show business, sport, politics, crime and so on. My particular inclinations were towards politics and crime. And after a few early successes working undercover posing as a drug dealer, I was quickly pigeonholed as a decent undercover operative.

My main piece of working equipment in those pre-digital days was a bulky but extremely high-quality Nagra tape recorder. These Swiss-made devices were favoured by many secret service outfits. Today, an undercover operative will have a tape recorder in his mobile phone or even in a pen. But in 1994, they were the size of four iPhones and had to be taped to your back, beneath your shirt. With this came the obvious danger of discovery. Villains tend to be very tactile people and the more alpha the male, the more likely he is to grab you in a big hug – and stumble across the tape recorder. I was often alone in these situations and the consequences could have been grave, so I always peddled the line that I was recovering from a severe shoulder injury. I even had a genuine ten-inch scar as evidence, from an earlier operation, should the need have arisen. Fortunately, it never did and in nearly twenty years of solid undercover work, I was never rumbled once, thankfully, as I adopted a variety of personae and cover stories to wheedle my way into gangs and into the lives of villains.

As well as building contacts leading to stories that would suit the paper and its readers, I felt I needed to quickly make my mark with a 'big hit'. A story that would make everyone's jaw drop.

The biggest story of 1994 was going to be the trial of Colin Stagg for the murder of Rachel Nickell, a young mother who was stabbed in front of her young son on Wimbledon Common. I was determined to get involved in it, either writing the backgrounder involving his family if he was found guilty or doing the first exclusive interview with Stagg if he was acquitted.

My involvement with the Rachel Nickell story was forged on the day of her death on 15 July 1992. I lived in Wimbledon at the time and had spent the morning strolling across the common with a girl called Jane, the girlfriend of an old girlfriend.

No more than a few hundred yards away, Rachel, a 23-year-old mother, was walking with her two-year-old son Alexander. She was stabbed forty-nine times and had her throat cut in front of her son before being sexually assaulted. The poor boy was found clutching his mother's bloodied body, repeating the phrase, 'Wake up, Mummy.' Few murders have so sickened and saddened a nation as this.

On *Today*, I had quickly made informal contact with the two leading detectives – Chief Inspector Mick Wickerson and Inspector Keith Pedder – who were leading the hunt and had collared Stagg. They were old-style policemen who didn't rely on press officers to tell them what they could and couldn't say to reporters. They simply relied on their judgement as to whether a reporter could be helpful to them and, if so, whether he could be trusted. I forged a very close – and very proper – relationship with them both quite quickly.

I had also got to know Stagg's mother Hilda Carr very well, to the point where she invited me to have tea with her in her terraced house in Putney, south-west London. Hilda, a straightforward lady, was good enough to give me exclusive access to the family background for a long period of time.

As Stagg's trial loomed in September 1994, I realised this story had the potential to be my first massive hit, just four weeks after joining the *News of the World*. At his Old Bailey trial, the police were judged to have set him up with an undercover policewoman and induced him to confess by suggesting to him that his involvement in the killing of Rachel was sexually thrilling to the policewoman, who was calling herself 'Lizzie James'. Although he was thirty at the time, Stagg was a virgin and, in his desperate naïveté, made some rash statements which had been taped, landing him in the dock, charged with Rachel's murder.

In fairness to the police, he bore an astonishing resemblance to the photofit picture of the chief suspect seen nearby, immediately after the killing. But that is about all one can say in their favour. Twenty years later, their crude entrapment seems of another age and from a dark corner somewhere behind the old Iron Curtain. When it was exposed in court, the judge threw out the case and Stagg walked free.

But for millions of people, the suspicion lingered that Stagg had walked on a technicality. In fact, to most people, Stagg was guilty and should have been locked up for life. He lived around the corner, walked his dog Brandy on the common every day, had a conviction for indecent exposure and had pagan effigies in his home. Add to that the photofit picture, and the man on the Clapham omnibus thought the most dangerous man in Britain had been freed to walk the streets and prowl Wimbledon Common.

Fleet Street wanted to write his story and the nation wanted to read it – even if it was through the gaps in their fingers covering their eyes.

I was confident enough to assure the news desk that my contacts with his family made me best placed on the paper to secure the interview. Only a few weeks into my job, they agreed to let me loose on it but under the watchful eye of Gary Jones, the paper's chief crime reporter. This was going to be the biggest story of the year and they were taking no chances.

Stagg's excellent barrister, Jim Sturman (now a QC), was my first point of contact; Stagg's mother, Hilda, my second. Letters and contracts from rival newspapers were flying into Sturman's London chambers. But Hilda's endorsement got us through the barrister's door and in pole position to clinch the deal. Sturman's position was firm, clear and fair. In the absence of any family endorsement for any other newspaper, I was the preferred reporter to do the interview. But he had to weigh that against the possibility that rival newspapers may be prepared to offer more money and therefore his client's best interests may eventually be served elsewhere.

Sturman conducted the auction, taking calls and hastily delivered letters throughout the day. Our advantage was that we were aware of the value of our rival's offers minute by minute as we sat drinking tea with Sturman and were in a position to better them at every turn. And while this was going on, I could tell Sturman was putting me quietly under the microscope and probing how I was going to cover the story.

By the end of the day, we clinched the deal for £40,000. We had our man and whisked him away to the Petersham Hotel in Richmond, Surrey, where I interviewed him at length. Stagg took his new girlfriend with him, Diane Beddoes, a 26-year-old woman who had written to him in prison. The following day, they revealed how Stagg had lost his virginity the night before, when they made love twice in the hotel room. Inexplicably, they also revealed how they had managed to break a sink in the process.

Stagg, an unsavoury character, appeared to me to be a dull man, obsessed with masturbation and professing to be the exact opposite of the psychological profile of the killer. Far from being a sadistic controller, Stagg claimed to prefer being dominated by women and to being attracted to female authority figures such as policewomen and the governess of Wandsworth Prison, where he'd been held. I could see no reason to doubt his claims, as he came across as shy, introverted and with a total lack of inclination to assert himself over any of the matters I confronted him with during our week together.

It was the story everyone wanted. But it was a fairly bland read, the essence of which was: 'I didn't do it, I can understand why they nicked me, I hope they catch the bastard who did it.' It was an interview every newspaper, broadsheet or tabloid, would have been glad to carry. But our story was to take a dramatic twist and produce one of the most memorable newspaper images of the 1990s.

The idea that transformed a run-of-the-mill, albeit greatly coveted, interview into a sensational exclusive came from Alex Marunchak.

One of the most controversial trials of one of the most horrifying murders in modern times had the nation divided. There were those who thought the police investigation was a shambles and Stagg was therefore plainly the wrong man. But there was a sizeable proportion who believed he was guilty and had been let off the hook on a technicality.

When I say the nation was divided, we had no scientific analysis to prove this was the case. As so often in journalism, you have to get a feel for the public mood. Good journalists have a sixth sense for this kind of thing – the public mood and its opinions on court verdicts, politicians, political parties, sportsmen and women, bands, singers etc. There are various weathervanes to assist in these areas, such as letters to the paper, opinion polls, pop charts, box office receipts, fan clubs, pressure groups, and comments made in restaurants and bars. Latterly, Twitter and YouTube have also proved excellent as a means of keeping an ear to the ground and weighing up the opinions of the great British public.

So it was through this process of social osmosis that we realised our readers that week would be divided on the guilt or innocence of Colin Stagg. In order to galvanise the divided public and harness them into one big five million-strong army of eager and expectant readers, a simple but ingenious idea by Marunchak was to put Stagg on a lie-detector machine and present the results to the reader with a graphic picture of Stagg wired to the machine.

One of the foremost experts of the lie detector, or polygraph, as it is known, is Jeremy Barrett, a former SAS officer who had taken his machine and knowledge to the USA, where it is admissible in a court of law.

Stagg was wired up to the machine with two straps across his chest and sensors on various parts of his body to detect minute changes of pulse, sweat output and tension across the chest and stomach.

Then the questioning began:

Barrett started gently at first, with three simple 'control' questions, the results of which were later compared against readings for controversial ones.

Q: Are you called Colin?

A: Yes.

Q: Is today Friday?

A: Yes.

Q: Are you in London?

A: Yes.

The machine needles whirred up and down, plotting a regular pattern.

Then Barrett threw in a trick question, designed to catch

out would-be liars.

> Q: Do you intend to answer truthfully the questions I'm about to ask you?
> A: Yes.

The polygraph whirred. Barrett raised the stakes.

> Q: Do you know who killed Rachel Nickell?
> A: No.
> Q: Did you walk on Wimbledon Common on July 15, 1992 [the day Rachel was killed]?
> A: Yes.
> Q: Have you ever masturbated on Wimbledon Common?
> A: Yes.
> Q: Did you ever see Rachel alive?
> A: No.
> Q: Do you suspect anyone of killing Rachel Nickell?
> A: No.
> Q: Were you on Wimbledon Common at approximately 10.15 a.m. on July 15, 1992?
> A: No.
> Q: Were you present when Rachel Nickell was killed?
> A: No.
> Q: Were you at home at approximately 10.15 a.m. on July 15, 1992?
> A: Yes.

The needles remained steady. Then, with no change in his calm, professional monotone, Barrett posed the crunch question.

Q: Did you kill Rachel Nickell?

The response was instant, the face expressionless, the voice calm and steady.

A: No.

The needles continued to whirr up and down showing not a flicker of anxiety.

The results were so conclusive, it took just two minutes for Barrett to decipher them and announce: 'You didn't kill Rachel Nickell.'

It took another fourteen years for Stagg to fully clear his name, but this was his first step. In 2008, a paranoid schizophrenic called Robert Napper, who had butchered another mother and her four-year-old daughter in 1993, pleaded guilty to Rachel's murder at the Old Bailey.

On 18 September 1994, the *News of the World* blazed the headline 'THE TRUTH! Exclusive. Rachel man Colin Stagg takes lie detector test for *News of the World*'. Pages 1, 2, 3, 4 and 5 were used to describe the test and announce his innocence, and to publish Stagg's interview with me. The front-page picture, although unintentional, made Stagg look as though he was strapped to the electric chair. It was dramatic tabloid fodder and was read by an astonishing 13 million people the following Sunday.

The one very tragic downside to the verdict and to the polygraph test was that Rachel's grieving family were now right back to square one, with no clue on the horizon as to who had killed this beautiful young mother.

Piers called me into his office at 8 p.m. on Saturday night when the paper hit the stands in King's Cross. The champagne was already poured. 'Well done. This calls for some serious fucking celebrating. You've scooped the entire street with this one. Is this the taste of things to come from you?'

There is no room for meekness in Fleet Street, and especially in front of Piers Morgan, who is constantly wreathed in chutzpah and emitting high-voltage super-confidence, which some find irritating but I have always found highly amusing. 'Yes, of course,' I boomed back, trying but failing to match his electricity. Disliking champagne and always hating the tense social gatherings in the editor's office on Saturday nights, I downed the drink, chatted for a few minutes then made some excuse about needing to take a phone call and left.

I'd been taken on at great expense as a big hitter and I'd landed my first big hit. I thought the huge weight of expectation would now lift from my shoulders, but I was wrong. I simply felt that I'd delivered what I was paid to do. And now I had to go out and do it again and again and again. But at least my confidence was high. And, most importantly, the news desk were to allow me free rein from now on, working solo on the stories of my choice.

CHAPTER 10

THE CASE OF THE DEVIL-WORSHIPPING POLICEMAN

AS I SETTLED into the bizarre and unpredictable lifestyle of an undercover *News of the World* reporter, it soon dawned on me that our readers came from a surprisingly wide cross-section of society.

We were shaped in the form of a downmarket, red-top Sunday tabloid. And yet many of our readers came from the professional classes. Lawyers, doctors and teachers numbered very highly among them.

But it was often a guilty habit, and one that was disguised. Professional readers would wrap up their *News of the World* in a copy of the *Sunday Times* to carry it home. One dentist who provided me with a few quotes for an article declared,

'Well, I never normally buy the *News of the World*, but I'll pick it up this weekend as you're quoting me.' Spotting a copy of that week's *News of the World* in his magazine rack, I fished it out and asked: 'I see. Who bought this?'

Blushing, he feigned surprise and mumbled something about his son having probably brought it back for the football results. A close inspection revealed the dentist's home address written in biro across the top of the newspaper, indicating he had it delivered weekly by his local newsagent. I nodded politely, ignoring the opportunity to demolish his pretence. But on the whole, the upper classes and upper middle classes tended to greet a *News of the World* reporter with a mixture of hospitality, fascination and curiosity.

The middle classes were generally a different kettle of fish and by far the trickiest to deal with, especially the lower middle class, which had perhaps worked hard to pull out their working-class roots. Members of these households would frequently complain that the father (or, most usually, the mother), had banned the publication from the house altogether. These same people would also frequently look down their noses at *Coronation Street* for the same reasons. We were a reminder of a grimy, working-class past, before their reincarnation as briefcase-carrying junior managers. With these people, a *News of the World* reporter was often regarded with fear and disdain.

Lower down the socio-economic ladder, the skilled and semi-skilled worker was less embarrassed about displaying their loyalties and, for as long as they could remember, we had been part of their household. Front-page stories from the 1940s and '50s were still vividly remembered. And for most, we were an essential part of their Sunday routine. To them, a *News of the World* reporter was regarded as a hero, and you would often find yourself being invited into a home merely to be paraded in front of a family audience of awestruck, dedicated readers by the fireside. 'Sunday wouldn't be Sunday without the *News of the World!*' was the commonly chanted greeting from them.

Despite our low-rent image, our marketing department discovered that we had more readers from groups A and B, the two top socio-economic groups, than *The Times* and the *Telegraph* combined. But we not only led the market at the 'popular' or 'low-brow' end, we actually dominated the entire market. During my time at the *News of the World*, only *The Sun* came anywhere near us.

One of the reasons for this was the paper's mixture of stories and themes and, above all else, revelations. Sensational revelations. For decades in the twentieth century, the paper's motto, displayed alongside the masthead, was 'All human life is there', taken from the Henry James line 'Cats and monkeys – monkeys and cats – all human life is there!', in his 1873 short story 'The Madonna of the Future'.

And it was the drama of human life, in all its vivid turmoil, tragedy, ecstasy, treachery, heroism, pomp and failure, that entertained our readers from 1843 until 2011. It was to prove a compelling mix for me, too. For, despite several entreaties from rival newspapers to join them, I was never remotely tempted to leave the *News of the World*.

Many of the stories that were covered by the *News of the World* simply aren't covered by newspapers any more. The bizarre tales of human behaviour have been relegated to the past, largely through reasons of privacy concerns, cost and the cooling effect of the Leveson Inquiry upon newspaper investigations.

I have selected a few to give example to this. Save in the most widely publicised cases or in cases of serious misdeeds, I will spare the blushes of most of the protagonists by keeping their names out of the narrative.

On 18 December 1994, I wrote a story headlined 'Top cop's Satan sex secret'. The introduction sums it up. 'A highly respected police [rank withheld] is a devil-worshipping pervert who takes part in sick sex acts during black magic rituals, the *News of the World* can reveal.'

The cast was an interesting one. There was the 'top cop', a very senior officer indeed, in charge of 300 policemen and women, married and aged forty-five. There was the children's social worker, aged fifty-eight, who was also head of his local village Neighbourhood Watch. There was the postman, aged thirty-five. Heading up the satanic sect was the evil high priest, 'John', a demonic, self-confessed sex maniac, local Tory activist and married father-of-two in his early fifties. There was a prostitute known as 'Samantha', an unhealthy-looking, undernourished girl in her mid-twenties, and a woman known only as 'Susan'. And there was me.

In those days, bizarre sects like this met each other through coded small ads in newspapers and contact magazines. Today, it would be on the internet. When I contacted 'John' through one such advert, he agreed to meet me in a small hut in the hollowed-out side of a hill in the countryside.

Here, I underwent a bizarre initiation ceremony, which involved me chanting a lot of mumbo-jumbo and swearing oaths of allegiance to Satan, with my shirt unbuttoned, my breast bared and my face set in a barely suppressed smile.

John stood just five and a half feet tall and had an impish, puckish look about him, with a black, bushy beard and deep-set eyes. He boasted, 'Being evil is a way of life for me. I've been a Satanist for as long as I can remember. Sex is all I think about.' He wanted to know if I could introduce any female members to the sect. I told him I could. Suddenly I was his new best friend.

The following week, I arrived for a satanic ritual with the assembled cast, bringing with me Sarah Courtenay, a very able *News of the World* freelance at the time. I also brought a bag with a hidden video camera inside it to capture the evidence.

Soon after everyone arrived at the hillside shrine, John announced that the police officer would be formally initiated into the sect. The officer was ordered to strip naked and was given the satanic name of Amon. He was then ordered to slit his elbow with a razor blade and smear blood on a piece of paper with his name written on it.

The paper was handed back to John, who warned the burly

policeman: 'This is a vow of secrecy. If you break it, you will be in severe trouble. We will get you.'

He then warned me: 'If you betray us, I will have you killed.'

As the sect chanted, John led the officer to the altar for his 'anointment'. As the policeman shouted 'Hail Satan' at the top of his voice, John dipped a dagger into a foul-smelling potion and dabbed the policeman's head, nipples and privates, screaming, 'May your wonderful body be always full of lust!'

John then produced an eighteen-inch black dildo (at the *News of the World* we were instructed to use the term 'sex aid', bizarrely). 'This is for the benediction,' he announced, using it once more to tap the nipples of the policeman, who by this time was beginning to look a little anxious as to where the outsized phallus might end up.

The policeman was then led to 'Susan' for the final part of the ceremony, 'the celebration of lust'.

Gaunt and naked, Susan fondled the policeman, who was by now grinning manically. And as the sect began chanting their mumbo-jumbo again, the policeman and the girl had sex on the altar surrounded by burning black candles.

After this depraved little episode, the social worker complained in the corner: 'No one here is gay like me, so there isn't any fun.'

My article records, in somewhat pantomime fashion: 'John's deep-set eyes lit up as he took a whip and beat slightly built [name withheld] around the shrine. The naked social worker leapt through the air screaming – apparently in ecstasy.'

Anyway, I think by now you've got the general picture!

Back at the office, I reviewed the tape with increasing dismay. A lot of work had gone into the story but I couldn't make out the features of the police officer. The ritual was carried out by candlelight and he appeared only as a dim and blurred figure. It looked like we wouldn't be able to expose him.

Then, out of the gloom, came the same lumbering figure who had minutes earlier been fornicating on the satanic altar. He was making a direct line for the video bag and stopped when he reached it, his beer belly being the only thing visible in shot by now. Slowly, the policeman lowered his face to inspect the expensive leather bag – which he appeared to admire – until his face finally came into full view. The job was done.

Nearly twenty years on, what lingers most in my memory was the calmness and total plausibility with which the policeman lied when I called him at his home to put the results of our investigation to him, or 'front him up', as we used to say. Despite having spent the best part of two hours in my company at the satanic ritual and having conversed with me before, during and after it, he flatly denied taking part in it. He said: 'This doesn't ring a bell. I'm sorry, I don't think I can talk about this. I'm getting most confused.' When told he was seen having sex with 'Susan', he became most indignant. 'Hang on, hang on! What are you talking about?' After showing him a picture clearly identifying him at the ritual, he shook his head and, with an amused smile, added: 'I'll take your word for it. I'm sorry but I don't know what you're on about.' I was absolutely certain of the evidence. But his bare-faced bluff unsettled me. Even when people are denying a story, usually their emotions betray them through some visible sign of anxiety. Only the genuinely innocent feel confident enough to brush aside utterly scandalous, career-threatening allegations with an amused grin.

We had a picture of him at the ritual and a picture of him talking to me at the door. They were both the same man. What we also needed was a picture of him in uniform to ensure all three matched up. If I'd asked the constabulary and told them I was from the *News of the World*, they would have wanted to know why. The reason – in order to expose one of their officers as a devil-worshipping pervert – would have seen the door slammed in my face. So I asked their local news agency (a group of local freelance journalists who offer reporting services to the media) to contact the constabulary for me. They were tasked to explain that they were writing a piece on the officer's recent promotion. The picture was sent over to them within the hour and then onto me. It left no doubt that the policeman and the 'devil-worshipping pervert' were one and the same man.

Soon after, he was removed from his job and, to this day, he remains the most plausible liar I have ever encountered.

We started the chapter by talking about why the *News of the World* was so successful, and I use this story as an indicator of why and how. That Sunday, I dropped into my local for a pint of bitter before our usual family lunch. The paper, as usual, was dotted around various tables. The pub attracted locals from all backgrounds, which was why I liked it. There was a plumber, a railway worker, an artist, some lawyers and several middle managers. They'd all read the story and were chortling (if they were men of the world) or sitting with mouths agape (if they weren't).

This is what the *News of the World* did week after week, on page after page, year after year, from 1843 to 2011.

The devil-worshipping policeman was no exception. It was indeed a sensational story that got the country into its usual frenzy of outrage and indignation, mixed with hilarity and incredulity.

But such was the *News of the World's* weekly embarrassment of riches to entertain the millions, it wasn't deemed strong enough for our front-page splash that week.

In fact, it was buried way back on pages 44–45 – the very last news pages in the paper.

CHAPTER 11

THE ROBIN COOK AFFAIR

ROBIN COOK'S AFFAIR with his secretary and mistress Gaynor Regan may never have come to light had he not been exposed so treacherously by one of his own. In an act of Machiavellian ruthlessness and duplicity, Cook's private life was torn apart and his wife humiliated by his Labour Party colleagues.

Since I broke the story in August 1997, I have never revealed how this story came to light. But in these days of post-Leveson analysis of the relationship between the press and politicians, there is no better example of the symbiotic connection that binds us. And there is no clearer picture, in my experience, of the moral turpitude that not only befogs Fleet Street but also swirls around the corridors of power in Westminster.

The final years of John Major's administration were punctuated by sex scandals that coined the phrase 'Tory sleaze'. This would prove the decisive nail in the coffin of an administration in turmoil with itself over Europe and in decline in the public's affections.

Labour stormed back into office with a landslide victory on 1 May 1997, ending eighteen years of Tory rule, inflicting the biggest defeat on the Conservatives since they were trounced by Campbell-Bannerman's Liberals in 1906.

With housewives' favourite Tony Blair at the helm, a majority of 179 under its belt and the air lambent with public hope and optimism, the newly centrist Labour held all the aces.

And yet, just ninety-four days into office, the new Labour government was rocked by a sex scandal far bigger than any seen during the years of Tory sleaze. And it was a crisis all of its own making.

Robin Cook was the new Foreign Secretary. A leading light in the Labour Party and highly regarded in the Commons for his outstanding intellect, Cook's star had never shone more brightly in the political firmament. In 1994, he had been widely tipped as a potential party leader on the death of John Smith but had ruled himself out as – bizarrely to some but astutely to others – 'too unattractive'.

But three years is a long time in politics and by 1997, it was no secret in Westminster that Cook was unhappy with Blair's lurch to the right. Many saw Cook as a potential left-wing successor if the wheel fell off the centrist bandwagon.

Few men have coveted the office of Prime Minister more than Gordon Brown. And most people in the Labour Party accepted as a foregone conclusion that Brown was Blair's natural heir should a vacancy arise in the near future. Hanging onto Brown's coat-tails were an army of scheming advisors and political allies whose sole aim was to ensure this remained the case. Their future professional ambitions were tied up with the fortunes of one man and the power of patronage he would hopefully one day inherit. It is this type of factionalism that so often results in Labour shooting itself in the head in public. And so it was with the Robin Cook affair. For the tip which exposed Cook came from within the party itself – from one of Gordon Brown's allies.

I shall say little about the identity of the informant, not because I am afraid of being contradicted or sued, but because, however unsavoury the individual, I have never betrayed a newspaper source. To a journalist, protecting sources is as sacrosanct as the Hippocratic Oath to a doctor. I readily accepted the tip, investigated it, wrote it and saw it published under my name on the front page of the *News of the World*. I accepted the treachery and the information it supplied at the time in order to fulfil my role as a newspaper reporter. So he earns my loyalty, though not my affection.

Tabloid newspaper informants are motivated by several factors. The most common include revenge, ambition, self-aggrandisement or financial gain. Some fall into the nobler category of 'whistleblower' and seek to correct an injustice or expose corruption. Even then, this is normally tied into an underlying, self-serving purpose of clearing their name or getting even with somebody. It is helpful to a journalist to establish pretty quickly what an informant's motivation for contacting him or her is as part of the delicate process of weighing up the quality of the evidence that supports their story.

Informants, or 'contacts', as they become known if they end up providing a regular stream of stories, are the lifeblood of journalism, however unedifying their motives may be.

The Robin Cook informant was motivated by ambition. Whether it was his ambition or the ambition of his boss Gordon Brown, the then Chancellor of the Exchequer, I have no way of telling. His seniority indicated a brief to operate unilaterally should he wish to do so, without the need to consult anyone. But it was a high-risk strategy. If it was ever revealed that he had tried to further the Chancellor of the Exchequer's leadership ambitions by discrediting the Foreign Secretary in such a brutal fashion, his career and that of Brown would have been damaged beyond repair.

So it was with some trepidation that the information was imparted, without any detail. 'Take a look at Robin Cook. You'll find something there. An affair.' That was all he gave up.

In politics, when an informant is knifing a colleague in the back, the whole process is so distasteful, even to them, that there is a tendency to try to distance themselves from the act of butchery. So rather than give you the full picture, they dispense a nod and a wink. And when the shocking scandal is exposed to the nation, they deceive themselves into believing it was the journalist who dealt the *coup de grâce* and not themselves. The same deluded thinking persuaded ancient tribes that unwanted children left to freeze on mountain sides were slain by the gods. On these occasions, the politician or advisor is the armourer and the journalist the gunman, and it is a relationship that has grown and flourished for over a century. At the Leveson Inquiry in 2012, Lord Justice Leveson was charged with analysing the relationship between the press and politicians but failed to reveal this type of relationship, upon which the great offices of state can be determined and which the press and politicians use to their mutual advantage.

So, armed with the only piece of evidence supporting an affair – 'Take a look at Robin Cook' – I set off to do just that. As Foreign Secretary, Cook had a grace-and-favour flat in Carlton Terrace and the run of Chevening, a magnificent 115-room country house in Kent. He also had a family home in Edinburgh, which he shared with his wife of twenty-eight years, Margaret. It seemed improbable that he would use the grace-and-favour properties for any liaison, as there would be too many ancillary workers milling around. And the family home was clearly off-limits.

Inside the House of Commons I had several useful contacts, one of whom helped me by discovering that Cook had a flat 'somewhere in the Victoria area'. But no address could be found. I decided to follow him home one night. When I was certain he was in the Commons, I had the main exit staked out by a motorbike encircling the roundabout directly outside. I remained at the main exit gate from the car park where

Cook would leave in the back of one of the chauffeur-driven Rovers.

Fortunately, the light June nights made it easier to spot him and soon after 10 p.m., the Rover carrying Cook sped out of the main gates and into light London traffic. I rang the nearby motorbike rider, who immediately picked him up and tailed him easily back to an address in Pimlico, just a few minutes away. Cook got out and the chauffeur helped him carry his red despatch boxes into a communal door serving a number of flats in a grand converted late Georgian, early Victorian house.

For a week, I watched Cook come and go from this flat. But he was always alone as he entered at night around 11 p.m, and he was always alone when he left in the morning, at around 8.15 a.m. If his mistress had entered or exited separately, it was impossible to tell. Several women came and went via the communal door but I had no way of knowing which flat they were visiting.

Faced with such early difficulties and with a paucity of evidence, the news desk decided to pull the plug. Greg Miskiw, the deputy news editor, said, 'We'll look at it again another time.' There were other, more immediate investigations on the go that I could lend a hand with. But when an investigation is put on the back burner, it is seldom resurrected unless further evidence surfaces. Normally, I was glad to be relieved from a long-shot, long-haul investigation, which could tie me up for weeks with no result. But this one was different. I requested a meeting with Miskiw and explained why I thought we should carry on.

There were two compelling reasons. The previous year, I had visited a Scottish landowner about two hours north of Edinburgh, who had a tale to tell. Sitting in the vast drawing room of his country house, designed in the Scottish Baronial style typical of the area, and overlooking thousands of acres of his spectacular estate, this was one contact who didn't sell me stories for money. He was extremely well connected and mixed freely among the elite in the worlds of both politics and business in Scotland.

His motivation was clear. He actively despised Cook, a sentiment I later learned was far from unique both north of the border and in Westminster. He disliked Cook's arrogance, pomposity and abrasiveness. The aristocracy are very good at rubbing along as equals with the working class, in a way that the middle classes aren't. But they can turn very spiteful if a middle-class upstart starts to talk down to them. And Cook, a man of few social graces, fell hopelessly into this category.

My source revealed that Cook had just finished a long-running affair with a mistress, and provided me with her name. He then added that Cook had been a serial philanderer for years, with dozens of mistresses and girlfriends all over the Scottish lowlands. He provided a further two names.

I had no reason to doubt this Scottish worthy. All things considered, I believed him. He even agreed to speak to one of the mistresses on the phone so I could listen in on an extension. Shy and reticent, she stopped short of confirming the relationship. But she didn't deny it either. But this wasn't enough to run a story and as all three ladies proved reluctant to help, the investigation was dropped.

A year later, however, it lent validity to the assertion from Gordon Brown's camp that Cook had a mistress, however improbable that sounded in a man frequently lampooned for his unfortunate resemblance to a garden gnome and his grating intellectual smugness.

The second compelling reason to continue with the investigation was that our latest source was a political heavyweight, giving us two impeccable sources. The first source had even provided names. This was no apocryphal story growing more outlandish and absurd with each telling. This was coming directly from the people who were working or associating very closely with him.

Miskiw wasn't convinced, so I came up with an unusual proposal. We should put two freelance photographers on the case and watch the flat 24/7.

Photographers Scott Tillen and Andy Tyndall were two of the finest operators on Fleet Street. They were an answer to every editor's prayer when it came to getting the picture. But their unique characteristic was their tenacity. They could be relied upon to sit outside an address fifteen hours a day, seven days a week for a month and never miss a moment's observation. They'd take it in relays to go to the lavatory or fetch food. Standing at 6ft 6in., Tillen was an unlikely undercover operative but one of the best I've known on a picture desk. Tyndall, an affable, bearded chap with a schoolmasterly air, was every bit his equal.

A deal was struck. Having convinced them of the quality of the informant, if not the quantity of the evidence, they agreed to give it six weeks' non-stop observation in return for £20,000 if their evidence ensured the story was published.

Weeks went by with nothing. Just the numerous flat residents coming and going, including Cook. But no sign of a woman entering or leaving with him.

After a month, the boys were becoming a little despondent. How did I know the tip was actually true? It was frustrating. If I told them who the informant was, they would have been stunned into a sense of sublime and unquestioning confidence. But I couldn't. The best I could offer was, 'Please just trust me guys. This is from the most senior of sources.' Luckily, they trusted my word and never wavered from their laborious task.

After five weeks, they spotted something unusual. Just before 8 a.m., Cook left his flat to put out the rubbish. But instead of walking back to the front door, he continued walking down the street in his shirt sleeves until he halted at a Renault Clio. After feeding the parking meter, he went home, put on his jacket and was picked up by his driver at 8.15 a.m.

An hour later, a middle-aged woman left the flats, got into the Renault Clio standing on the meter and drove off. The boys followed it as she drove north, ending up at a house in Charlbury, Oxfordshire, keeping me updated on the phone as they desperately tried to keep up with her and yet remain unseen. If Cook had fed the meter and the car belonged to a woman, perhaps this was his overnight guest? And perhaps the overnight guest was the mistress?

I did a quick electoral roll check on the house and found the woman living there was Gaynor Regan. Another quick check with my contacts at the House of Commons revealed she was Robin Cook's secretary. Further checks with neighbours revealed she had split up with her husband Stephen about three years previously.

For several days, Tillen and Tyndall kept up their watch to ensure Gaynor's presence was not simply a one-off, and it quickly became apparent Cook and Regan were living together as a couple during the week. I wrote the story and on the Friday before publication, the editor, Phil Hall, put the allegations to Tony Blair's press secretary Alastair Campbell.

Campbell recalls the moment in his book *The Blair Years*, published in 2007.

On 1 August 1997, he writes: 'I got a message to call Phil Hall at the *News of the World*. I said I hope you are not going to unleash a scandal while I am on holiday. He said no, I'm going to do it now. I said what? He said: "Robin and Gaynor."'

On hearing the paper had evidence of the affair, Campbell went to Blair and announced: 'I bring you your first sex scandal.'

They discussed whether Cook would have to resign – and whether they could replace him.

'TB and I then went round the entire Cabinet thinking of skeletons we either knew of, or could imagine. I said if you're not careful you'll be left with [Scottish Secretary Donald] Dewar and [Transport Minister Gavin] Strang.'

Campbell managed to contact Cook, who was in a car on his way to Heathrow Airport to go on holiday with his wife Margaret. He told him that the affair would soon be made public.

'I could now hear Margaret chatting away happily in the background. I said are you sure you don't want to find a private phone. He said no, you speak, and I will listen. I was, I must say, quite impressed at how cool he was.'

Cook told his wife immediately and cancelled his holiday. The next day he announced he was leaving her for Gaynor, whom he married in 1998.

Cook's brutal indifference to the feelings of his wife of twenty-eight years and the mother of his two sons is still shocking to read.

A clearer view of the emotional turmoil Cook, Campbell and Blair created through their 'management' of their response came from Margaret Cook. In a searing response to Campbell's memoir, she wrote a first-person piece for the *Daily Mail* on 12 July 2007 under the headline 'The day Alastair Campbell killed my marriage to Robin Cook'.

She said:

> Try to imagine driving to the VIP lounge at Heathrow, reserved only for the great and the good, en route to a gloriously restorative holiday in Boston.
>
> A holiday that was to celebrate the renewed joy you had

in your marriage – one which seemed to be on track again after a decidedly rocky patch.

This was my situation some ten years ago.

Robin Cook, my then husband, Foreign Secretary no less, was taking longer than me to unwind, and at about 4 o'clock on the afternoon of August 1, his mobile rang.

In my euphoria, I did not let this annoy me. I was so used to blocking out Robin's tension that I ignored it. But I must have registered something unusual. He said very little, in a clipped, stern voice.

As I later found out, in those few minutes and in that one-sided conversation the fate of my marriage was decided by a political machine without grace or empathy; not just the blind, line-toeing obedience to the political good of the party, but egocentric male-manoeuvring for position on the greasy pole.

Though I have thought about this day many times, I have never heard the other side of that telephone conversation, the words of the man known for his bullying tactics who colluded with my husband in reaching the decision that was for me, so shattering – for them, merely convenient.

Alastair Campbell recalls in his newly published diaries how he discovered that Robin was conducting an affair with his secretary Gaynor Regan.

When a tabloid paper was poised to reveal the affair, Campbell called Robin with – I guess – the usual code-speak that passes for a dire threat in political circles. Certainly, that was how Robin read the Campbell intimations.

In his book, even Campbell comments on Robin's coolness when he took the call, talking over the phone as I sat next to him in the car, in a 'weird kind of code' – to me it sounded like monosyllables.

You'd think I'd have picked up on it, but at the time I was oblivious. I'd never been the suspicious, jealous, possessive sort of wife that has her sensors on alert all the time.

Campbell claims in the book, and I can even now feel my shoulders tensing with the horror of this revelation, that Robin actually asked for his advice. But I know now what was streaking through Robin's mind. How do I limit the damage to *myself*?

He was trying to mind-read, to work out which way would gain him the most sympathy with his political master. Wife or mistress?

Rightly, Campbell did not help him. But both were thinking of Tory Ministers, who tended to drop the mistress like a hot potato and wheel out the supportive and tenacious family. That hadn't worked for David Mellor or Cecil Parkinson, though. Hmmm…

This week is the first time I've heard Campbell's account of the Heathrow Airport episode that ended my marriage.

Despite the press stories at the time, I never actually accused him of telling Robin to break up with me. Of course, he didn't do anything so crass; the devil would be in the detail, the nuances, the subtle and understated threats.

I was naive about the cut-throat world of which I was on the periphery, but I knew enough to understand that Robin must act in such a way as to cause the least trouble to Blair, otherwise he would lose his job as Foreign Secretary.

They knew that the unstated threat would be enough to bring him to heel. Campbell's account in his book of how they chewed over who could be Foreign Secretary if all went pear-shaped, shows how close to the wind Robin was sailing.

And I knew that this was the matter uppermost in his mind, not an emotional choice between Gaynor – the other woman – and me. And this was the source of the greatest heartache for me, that Robin could be so cold and clinical and calculating as that terrible day unfolded.

We had been together for more than thirty years, had been at the heart of a loving family, had been excellently good friends through most of that time – and yet I received so little compassion from him.

In his recollection of that day, Campbell says that after the car-phone conversation had been cut off by loss of signal, Robin came back 'a few minutes later' and also spoke to Blair.

We had reached the VIP lounge with the retinue, and Robin had been ferociously rude to everyone, telling them abruptly to get out. Then he briefly told me about the *News of the World* story of him and Gaynor, and that the holiday was cancelled because he couldn't leave the country, and that he thought we should part. Just like that.

Robin was never good at dealing with emotional tension, and he was probably relieved to get it off his chest. I was so stunned I was more or less speechless for a while, and I certainly didn't break down at that stage.

I don't recall Robin being emotional at all, and it was then that I realised in retrospect how cold he had been on the phone in the car when talking to Campbell, and that just seemed to continue.

He was like an alien. I asked him then: 'Will you lose your job?' and I remember to this day the intolerable smugness with which he said: 'Oh no, I shan't lose it' and how at that juncture, I realised that my marriage was slipping away. I was no longer needed, I was an impediment.

Campbell comments, too, in his diaries that Robin was far more concerned about Gaynor than about me.

In the hours after the first phone calls, time seemed to have no meaning. I was devastated and befuddled. More calls were made, staff sent off to collect our luggage from the Boston flight, which had no doubt been held up.

Tickets were bought for me to return to our home in Edinburgh. Someone was even despatched to change my phone number so the press would not hound me too much.

I rallied enough to decide to go into London with Robin, at least to make a last-ditch attempt to retrieve my life.

According to Campbell, there was a later phone call, when

I was not present, in which Robin said to Blair that the Gaynor thing was more than a fling, more than a romance. Again I imagine Robin was feeling his way, nosing out the reaction and testing for sympathy.

Certainly he knew that if he stayed with me he would have more bridges to build, more apologies, more sackcloth and ashes, more sins to expiate. And perhaps there was the thought that I might be the more dignified loser.

However, I note one shocking lie in the new book, presumably originating from Robin.

Campbell claims that Robin told Blair we had not been 'man and wife' for some time and he had been trying to finish the marriage. That was blatant self-preservation. We'd had a restoration of our loving relationship for some months past, and the cancelled holiday was supposed to be a celebration of that fact.

One can only conclude he thought he could get away with keeping wife and mistress – and that somehow no one would notice.

The negotiations Campbell records over the press announcement are accurate enough. I did indeed insist that Robin say: 'I am leaving my wife.' I was emphatically not going to let them spin the line that I was giving the break-up my blessing.

It seems to me now that Robin's cruelty and neglect, with which his colleagues – including Campbell – concurred, was a way of making himself feel I was guilty of something

154

or other and getting my just deserts. It is a stereotyped way for erring men to justify themselves.

Finally, there was a letter of consolation from Tony Blair. I have it still. It says nothing consolatory about anything except being in the eye of the media storm; nothing about hopes for my future. No such empathy from New Labour.

The Masters were satisfied with Robin's performance, and he was never in any danger of losing his job. That speaks volumes.

Any half-decent man would expect him under those circumstances to give his wife top priority, to go away on holiday as planned and at least let her down in a dignified and considerate way. Even if it endangered his career.

New Labour thugs lost sight of what ordinary people perceive as courtesy and decency.

The worst Alastair Campbell says about me in his book is that I was a cow (for dictating to Robin what he should do), and he reports that I was later described as 'f*****g ghastly' by an on-message focus group who called 'Shagger Cook' a hero (this all emerged at the time my memoirs were published in 1999).

In Campbell's single-minded crusade to protect his boss's image, I was unwittingly a huge embarrassment (although an innocent bystander), so I suppose that's quite mild, coming from him.

On the one occasion he met me, he didn't take to me, he now writes. Oh really? That's a bit thin for spin, but, of course, it's not true. We didn't meet, or if we did it was so unmemorable as to be a non-event.

Yet it is odd that I never met or even spoke to someone who fingered my life so ruthlessly and dispassionately.

All that was ten years ago, almost to the day; a new lifetime ago, so refreshingly different and happy that I'm not even emotional about going over the story again.

I don't have any smouldering resentment towards Campbell – he's not worth it.

The simple truth is that he was part of an unsavoury political machine. But he was only a fixer. A temporary one at that.

What is striking is what a disorganised, amateurish, crazy way to run a country theirs was. And worse, to write about it afterwards.

As the tragic domestic drama played out, Cook and his staff prepared a statement, which read:

I can confirm that I am leaving my wife. I want to make it clear that the responsibility for this is entirely mine.

Margaret and I now hope to restructure our lives. Throughout my political career I have tried to keep my family out of the public eye. I deeply regret that this will cause such distress to them.

I will have no further statement to make on this matter and those involved have no wish to make any comment. I accept that I am a public figure but I would ask for the privacy of those involved to be respected at a very painful time.

This was quickly followed by Tony Blair's expression of sorrow, issued by Campbell. It read:

> The Prime Minister is very sorry for Robin and Margaret and he feels for all concerned.
>
> He sees this as a personal tragedy for those involved which does not affect Robin Cook's capability as a truly outstanding Foreign Secretary.
>
> While in an ideal world, all marriages would be lasting, the truth is that these situations do arise and he hopes that Robin and Margaret can be left to rebuild their lives.

On Sunday 3 August 1997, the *News of the World* splashed with my story: 'World Exclusive: Cabinet Minister and His Secret Love'. It was to make headlines all over the world. The story also got me my first nomination for an award, for Scoop of the Year at the 1998 British Press Awards. In the event, I was pipped at the post by the *Mirror*'s James Whitaker for his exclusive revelation that Princess Diana had fallen in love with a young man by the name of Dodi Fayed. It was a very worthy winner.

No one apart from Margaret Cook came out of the sorry saga with any dignity. The Gordon Brown camp showed their hideous tactics to further their own ambitions; Blair and Campbell their psychopathic disregard for the emotional fallout; Robin Cook the truly unforgivable callousness to his wife at the airport.

Even my own newspaper showed itself to be disingenuous. High up in the story, in paragraph seven of the three-page story, the following words were inserted: 'Their relationship had been brought to our attention by two freelance photographers who spotted the pair sharing what appeared to be a domestic life together at his London flat.'

No mention that we had been tipped off by Gordon Brown's camp. No mention that we had tasked the two photographers to aggressively target the Foreign Secretary. We didn't want to dirty our hands with that and find ourselves sidelined by a very powerful new Labour government.

The Brown camp was delighted. They had neutralised their main rival for the great office of Prime Minister. And we were delighted because it gave us the first big scandal involving New Labour.

Such is the relationship between the press and politicians that Lord Justice Leveson failed to reveal. 'Twas ever thus. And it will always be so. However distasteful he finds it and however much he tries to regulate it, he will never change the nature of the political beast and the Fleet Street jungle he inhabits.

CHAPTER 12

THE JEFFREY ARCHER EXPOSÉ

THE EXPOSURE AND jailing of Jeffrey Archer for perjury and perverting the course of justice after a *News of the World* investigation was one of our strongest stories of the 1990s.

Nailing Archer for the crook that he was had been something of a Fleet Street Holy Grail for over a decade.

In 1986, we had exposed Archer, the Conservative Party deputy chairman, for paying off a prostitute called Monica Coghlan. Our tape-recorded call between Coghlan and Archer left no room for manoeuvre and he quit.

But the *Daily Star* went one step further and followed up our story by saying what everyone was thinking but we couldn't prove or print – that he had been paying her for sex too.

Archer took the *Daily Star* to court and won £500,000 damages from them after lying through his teeth. The editor of the *Daily Star*, Lloyd Turner, was sacked, and died a few years later aged just fifty-seven, 'a broken man, with his reputation in tatters', according to his widow Jill.

Everyone on Fleet Street knew Archer to be a liar and an elaborate embroiderer of the truth. But after the colossal damages he had received, he had acquired a Teflon reputation and editors were afraid to take him on again.

Despite the reservations of Fleet Street and the private warnings of Tory grandee Edward du Cann, Archer remained a favoured golden boy among the party elite. And by 1999, he was running as the Conservative Party's candidate in the forthcoming Mayor of London elections – with the endorsement of Lady Thatcher and the then party leader William Hague.

Archer once again swaggered onto the stage, full of the usual braggadocio, and Fleet Street clenched its collective teeth. Nothing, it would seem, could be done to stop this man.

Suddenly, a man called Ted Francis, a 68-year-old former TV producer and friend of Archer, paid a visit to the publicist Max Clifford with an extraordinary claim. He had agreed to fake an alibi for the night it was claimed Archer had sex with Coghlan. Archer was a perjurer. He shouldn't be running for Mayor of London. He should be jailed, Francis claimed.

Max handed him on to my editor, Phil Hall, who immediately saw how sensational the allegations were and called a meeting with myself and Greg Miskiw, who was then news editor. Phil was incredibly relaxed. He had no doubt the story was true. But in order to prove it, we would have to have evidence of the highest calibre. Nothing less than a full, taped confession would suffice. And he doubted we would be able to get it now. Archer would be on his guard. And there had been a minor falling-out between the two men, so contact would be difficult. 'Let's have a chat with him and see what he has to say,' were Phil's parting words.

I jumped into my car and motored down to Cranleigh in Surrey, relieved that this Mission Impossible wasn't carrying with it the added burden of unrealistic expectations. With hindsight, it was a shrewd move on Phil's behalf, as it allowed me to approach the whole complex business with a cool, calm, clinical eye. And within half an hour of talking to Francis, I realised this had the potential to be not only the biggest story of the decade but also one of the easiest.

Francis claimed publicly that his motivation to expose Archer sprang from his desire to prevent a crook becoming Mayor of London. But he confided privately that it was a particularly crass public put-down that had turned him against his former friend.

Archer had advanced Francis £12,000 to help mount a new production of Enid Blyton stories for TV and had later cancelled the debt.

Francis needed £100,000 for the project and Archer promised a £25,000 investment. But when Francis collected his promised money from the bank it was £12,000.

Francis said Archer told him the money was a gift not a loan, saying: 'I don't expect to see this back, you know.'

However, the arrangement was eventually to sour their

friendship. Francis was invited to one of Archer's famous 'champagne and shepherd's pie' gatherings in his penthouse overlooking the Thames in 1990.

He was approached by Archer as he was chatting to an actress and Archer delivered a humiliating put-down. He said: 'You want to watch this man, you know. I lent him £20,000 once and I'm still waiting to get the money back.'

Francis said: 'She was dreadfully embarrassed and I was deeply hurt. For a start it was untrue, it was only £12,000, and it was an investment, not a loan. He humiliated me in front of my peers. I didn't understand why.'

Ted Francis is an immensely likeable man with an affable nature. But this had made his blood boil. Very much of the old school, he felt his honour had been besmirched.

To nail Archer, there were two hurdles to overcome. Firstly, how did we get Francis to put in a call to Archer, a man whom he had fallen out with, without arousing suspicion? Secondly, how did we get Archer to confess?

I worked out a formula working backwards from the result we needed. The result we needed was for Archer to 'remind' Francis on the phone as to the precise nature of the illegal conspiracy they had entered into thirteen years previously, when Francis had acted as an alibi, thereby incriminating himself.

This would be difficult for a variety of reasons. Why should Francis want or need to be reminded of the details of a long past conspiracy? Why would Archer want to incriminate himself on the phone to a former friend whom he had fallen out with over a minor disagreement? What reason could Francis have for contacting Archer in the first place?

The solution came to me in a matter of minutes. The journalist Michael Crick, then at the BBC, had long been investigating Archer tenaciously and had become something of a thorn in his side. He was thorough, persistent and also very, very good at his job. Archer was rattled by him.

This gave me the key to unlock the first door. Why should Francis call Archer about the false alibi and why would Archer want to listen to him and discuss it with him? I instructed Francis, with the help of a script, to claim that Crick had been in touch with him and was in possession of information which could potentially expose Archer's attempt to pervert the course of justice. That got Archer listening immediately.

The second component of the telephone call was for Francis to get some of the details wrong about the false alibi conspiracy so Archer would step in and correct him, thereby incriminating himself.

It worked. Archer walked straight into the trap and the tape was played back at his Old Bailey trial, sinking him.

Here's what was said. The men are discussing the false alibi, which is a letter sent by Francis to Archer's lawyers, claiming the two men were having dinner together on the night Archer was meant to have had sex with Coghlan. (In the end, the alibi wasn't needed as the date in question was changed – but the offence of attempting to pervert the course of justice had been committed with the sending of the letter.)

TABLOID SECRETS

4 NOVEMBER 1999 AT 5.15 P.M.

FRANCIS: Have you had Michael Crick on the phone to you?

ARCHER: No.

FRANCIS: Well, he's been on to me a couple of times and he's cracking on about the letter that I wrote to Mishcon [Archer's lawyer]. Do you remember?

ARCHER: No.

FRANCIS: Right, there were two. I thought at first it was the letter I'd written about the J thing. C. J.

ARCHER: C. J., remind me?

FRANCIS: There was that suit going on and he was trying to sue you and K. E., the thing that fell through. It was all a lot of fuss about nothing. But apparently it wasn't. That's not the letter he's on about. He was on about a letter I wrote on the 22nd of January. I'm saying that because I've got a copy of it in front of me, in 19…

ARCHER: (interrupting) Yup, how did he get a copy of it?

FRANCIS: I don't know. He hasn't got a copy of it as far as I know.

ARCHER: Good.

FRANCIS: I'm talking about a copy I had on my file.

ARCHER: Well, how did he get a copy? How does he know about it?

FRANCIS: I don't know. I've no idea.

ARCHER: Jesus, what does it say?

FRANCIS: It's the one about the alibi.

ARCHER: Oh, Christ. Am I asking you to do something?

FRANCIS: Yeah.

ARCHER: Oh, Christ. Read it to me.

FRANCIS: (reads the letter)

ARCHER: Do you think he [Crick] has a copy of that?

FRANCIS: I don't know.

ARCHER: I don't think he does, Ted.

FRANCIS: He knows about the letter.

ARCHER: Yeah, well don't ever let him see it. It's the wrong day though, isn't it?

FRANCIS: Well, yeah. He says that there was some confusion over the dates of the 9th of September.

ARCHER: Correct. And then we got the dates right and your letter did not affect...

FRANCIS: And did not have any...

ARCHER: ... effect at all.

FRANCIS: No.

ARCHER: So I would be obliged if, I mean you know how this man is, just never let him see it. Most of my friends now, Ted, are refusing to take his calls full stop.

FRANCIS: You see, originally I thought it was quite innocuous because I thought it was about the C. J. thing when he first mentioned letters to Mishcon.

ARCHER: Yah.

FRANCIS: We all know that that then passed under the bridge.

ARCHER: But you've never given him a copy of this letter?

FRANCIS: No, Christ no, no, no.

ARCHER: How does he even know about it then?

FRANCIS: I don't know. Did you ever mention it?

ARCHER: No. Not that I'm aware of.

FRANCIS: … then we had dinner there, didn't we?

ARCHER: We did.

FRANCIS: Sambuca.

ARCHER: Sambuca.

FRANCIS: That's it.

ARCHER: At that little restaurant.

FRANCIS: And Ernie Saunders walked in.

ARCHER: Correct.

FRANCIS: It all came flooding back to me.

ARCHER: What a good memory you have.

FRANCIS: And I remember you saying to me, 'Look – meet the maître'd and the waiter so they recognise you' and I remember saying to you, 'Well, they'll recognise me anyway because I have bloody well eaten here before.'

ARCHER: (laughs)

FRANCIS: And then you said to me, 'What were you doing on September the 9th last year?' And I said, 'Buggered if I know.' You said, 'We had dinner here, didn't we?' And I said, 'Well, if you say so.' Do you remember?

ARCHER: Yeah, but we have got to be careful, Ted. We don't want to go to [a] court of law with this.

FRANCIS: No, I mean how the hell could he have found out?

ARCHER: Well, if you haven't given him the letter, he can't have found out.

FRANCIS: The only one I would have mentioned it to would have been I. A. Do you remember I. A.?

ARCHER: I remember I. A. But you wouldn't have given him the letter.

FRANCIS: Oh no, bloody hell!

ARCHER: Well then, Ted, my best bet is please just refuse to take his calls.

FRANCIS: All right. You see what I'm worried about? I don't want to see it in the public domain.

ARCHER: No, of course not.

FRANCIS: And most of all, I don't want my family to find out that I told a porkie because you know what it's like with family?

ARCHER: Well, there's no proof that this is a porkie.

FRANCIS: No.

ARCHER: In my diary, it's fifteen years ago.

FRANCIS: Have you got your diary for that?

ARCHER: Yes.

FRANCIS: Is my name in it?

ARCHER: Oh, yes, oh yes.

FRANCIS: Because I looked in my diary and I could not see what the bloody hell I was doing.

ARCHER: No, no. You're down there. Dinner with me.

FRANCIS: On September 9th?

ARCHER: Yup.

FRANCIS: Oh, that's all right then. OK, well, look, forgive me for ringing.

ARCHER: No. No. Thank you. But you know, he's just a destructive influence. A. just told me he had a call from him and just put the phone down.

FRANCIS: Right. OK. I'm puzzled about how he found out. You wouldn't have told anyone, would you?

ARCHER: Certainly not. Certainly not, Ted.

FRANCIS: I was going to ask him if he got it from K., because K's the only common link between...

ARCHER: But if you talk to him, you give him a name. You then give him K., he rings K.

FRANCIS: But it was K. who put him onto me.

ARCHER: Well, don't mention any names to him. Don't talk to him.

FRANCIS: All right.

ARCHER: Thanks, Ted.

9 NOVEMBER 1999 AT 6.15 P.M.

ARCHER: Ted.

FRANCIS: Jeffrey, I am sorry to bother you again.

ARCHER: Not at all.

FRANCIS: This bloody business is getting rather heavy now.

ARCHER: But I thought you were just going to put the phone down on him.

FRANCIS: Well, I was, but now Crick's saying that he knows for certain that we cooked up that alibi.

ARCHER: Ted, he does not know – he is trying to get you to say you know.

FRANCIS: But he has given me the evidence – or he's told me about the evidence.

ARCHER: And what is the evidence?

FRANCIS: He says that I was at the Grand Hotel in Brighton and that he has got, what do you call it, one of my credit card receipts for it. I couldn't remember and now it has all come back to me.

ARCHER: Oh, good God, that's interesting.

FRANCIS: I was there with a guy called John and I don't know whether Crick has spoken to him or not. But we went down there to see his girlfriend, who is working as a nurse.

ARCHER: Oh right.

FRANCIS: And that is why it has all come back.

ARCHER: But that night is not relevant.

FRANCIS: Which night?

ARCHER: The night that we were meant to have been at that restaurant.

FRANCIS: Oh, the September the 9th…

ARCHER: … was not the night that I'm meant to have seen the girl.

FRANCIS: Oh right.

ARCHER: They are not even connected.

FRANCIS: So are you saying…

ARCHER: Didn't you realise that?

FRANCIS: No.

ARCHER: Oh gosh. Oh, I am sorry, Ted, you have been through all this, I apologise.

FRANCIS: Oh God.

ARCHER: It is a different day.

FRANCIS: So, why did we cook up the alibi?

ARCHER: Because they changed the day and then they changed it back.

FRANCIS: And you were covering?

ARCHER: Yes. I am so sorry you didn't realise.

FRANCIS: Because I was thinking perhaps I ought to get hold of J. and say, 'Look, if you haven't spoken to this guy X, put the phone down on him.'

ARCHER: Yes, you'd better tell him to do that. But it is not the day that is relevant. It is totally irrelevant. What happened was, let me take you through it slowly. They got the wrong day. So I was having dinner in that restaurant that night … the Sambuca, on the day they thought.

FRANCIS: That was the 9th.

ARCHER: Yes. It was with someone else and that was the only reason. I certainly did have dinner there that night. There is no doubt that I had dinner there that night. If they got the restaurant booking, they would find that I had dinner there that night. It was not with you. It was with another person. Then the defence said, 'Oh, sorry, it wasn't that day you were with the prostitute, it was the next day, which was in fact the day I was in the Caprice with Richard Cohen [Archer's literary editor].

FRANCIS: Oh, I remember that.

ARCHER: And when we went to trial, the reason why you

weren't in the trial was because it wasn't the day that you were affected. You weren't anything to do with it.

FRANCIS: Oh, I needn't have written to the lawyer.

ARCHER: No, you needn't have written at all. Absolutely irrelevant.

FRANCIS: OK. Thank God for that.

ARCHER: No, no. It's totally and completely irrelevant today. Now it's possible he's found out you were not with me on the day you thought you were. That's possible. But it's not relevant, Ted.

FRANCIS: So even if he says, 'Ted Francis cooked up this alibi with Jeffrey for that...'

ARCHER: He can't say you cooked up that alibi. He can't say we cooked up that alibi. You could sue him for that. But I wouldn't speak to him.

FRANCIS: Should I get onto J.?

ARCHER: Yes please and ring me back and tell me what happens.

FRANCIS: OK.

ARCHER: Tell me if he has got onto him.

FRANCIS: OK. That's if I can find him. He's left the district. But I will go through sources.

ARCHER: But I definitely had dinner that night at that restaurant. It wasn't with you. The following night was when all the action took place and that is why you didn't go to court. You didn't go to court because it was irrelevant. You weren't part of it. It didn't matter where you were the night before. You could have been in Timbuktu.

FRANCIS: And there was me cursing the day I ever wrote the letter.

ARCHER: Yes, it is irrelevant. And you genuinely may have made a mistake about where you were on that night. But don't talk to him because every time you talk to him you give him ammunition.

FRANCIS: I won't talk to him ever again.

ARCHER: Good.

FRANCIS: Have a good evening.

ARCHER: You too. I'm sorry, you would have been in court, Ted, had it been the night that mattered.

FRANCIS: I know and I don't have a spare pair of brown trousers unfortunately.

ARCHER: Ha, ha, ha … no, it doesn't involve you in any way.

ARCHER RINGS FRANCIS ON 9 NOVEMBER 1999 AT 7 P.M.
HIS WIFE SAYS HE IS IN THE BATHROOM AND WILL RING
BACK TWO MINUTES LATER.

ARCHER: Ted, even if he has traced your American Express card, and God knows how he's done that, why alert Mr X and let him in on the game?

FRANCIS: Yeah, although John is an old friend.

ARCHER: Yeah.

FRANCIS: I could imagine … well, I don't want to be unfair to him … but if I were to say to him, 'Look, this is the status quo. You may be contacted by a freelance journalist and he will talk about you and I being together in the Grand Hotel in Brighton…'

ARCHER: That night.

FRANCIS: ... that night and I happened to have cooked up an alibi for Jeffrey...

ARCHER: And that would be terrible.

FRANCIS: ... and he would turn round and say ... 'Well, I am not going to tell a lie – you can tell lies for your friends if you like, but I am not going to tell lies to you although we are old friends, because you know I am not like that.'

ARCHER: Quite right – that is fair enough. That is fair enough, Ted ... now we go onto the next stage because Crick thinks he has got a story of course because he thinks you have told a lie, which he can now prove and therefore I have told a lie because I was saying that you were at Sambuca with me when you weren't.

FRANCIS: Right.

ARCHER: There is a good side and a bad side to this. The good side is that I was at Sambuca, that's the good side, i.e. my alibi, I was at Sambuca, is fine. The fact that I got it wrong who I was with is incidental in a way, if you think about it. Because it is where I was which matters not who I was with.

FRANCIS: What about the letter I wrote to the lawyer?

ARCHER: What letter did you write? Oh yes, saying you were at Sambuca...

FRANCIS: With you...

ARCHER: He claims he has got that letter, does he?

FRANCIS: Yes.

ARCHER: I wonder how he got that?

FRANCIS: He is saying, 'You lied for Jeffrey Archer.'

ARCHER: Yes.

FRANCIS: That is what he is saying.

ARCHER: Right.

FRANCIS: And I sort of, I couldn't very well turn round and say, 'Well yes, that's true.'

ARCHER: No, no.

FRANCIS: Anyway, you were saying.

ARCHER: Well, we have got to think this through more carefully. One, I don't think your man [John] comes on the scene because I doubt if he keeps a diary. I doubt if he remembers. I doubt if he remembers who paid the bill. I mean, it's fifteen years ago. So I don't suppose he can remember he was at a Brighton hotel with you on that day. Unless he also paid for a bill.

FRANCIS: No, I paid for the meal there.

ARCHER: Fine.

FRANCIS: If you were to say to him or anyone, 'Where were you on the 9th...'

ARCHER: Oh ... anyone ... last week.

FRANCIS: '... 1986', they would say, '1986, you are kidding.'

ARCHER: Yeah, that is fourteen years ago, thirteen years ago. It is 9th September. Well, now the date that matters is the 10th September. That is the date that matters. [In fact, Archer himself gets the date wrong here.] September 10th is when it all happened. They got the date wrong and then they changed it halfway through to the correct date, the

174

10th. So the 9th is a total irrelevance. To prove the 9th is a total irrelevance, you would have been in the witness box for two days if the 9th was the real date, are you with me?

FRANCIS: Yes.

ARCHER: Instead, all those people who were there on the 10th were all in the witness box, one after the other.

FRANCIS: So where did the 8th come into it?

ARCHER: You'll never believe this. The man who accused me of being there had the wrong diary. He had a 1985 instead of a 1986 diary and he wrote it on the wrong date. He then changed it three months later to the correct day.

FRANCIS: This is the man on the other side of the fence?

ARCHER: Yeah. And so then you became irrelevant. Because you were no longer a witness at any level. Because your day didn't matter.

FRANCIS: I get it now. That's why you wanted me to write the letter in the first place because…

ARCHER: … because he changed the day and I was at the restaurant but not with someone I would want the world to know I was with, er…

FRANCIS: I know.

ARCHER: Yep … who was nothing to do with the business at all but I didn't need it out in the open.

FRANCIS: Of course. It is a much more personal affair.

ARCHER: Absolutely. Much more.

ARCHER AND FRANCIS CONTINUE TO DISCUSS THE LETTERS SENT TO MISHCON.

ARCHER: Yes, I think it was irrelevant by then. Frankly, I think we knew then they had changed the date. Now all they have got, and I apologise for this, Ted, all these years later, I apologise, all they have got is you lying and therefore they will try and prove me to be a liar. So they may well print your letter to the, I can see *The Guardian* saying, 'Look, he said this and he wasn't even there.' The good news is I was there. I don't have to say who I was with but I was there and that is fine. What we got wrong was who I was with. But there is no question, you know, I wasn't in Scotland, I wasn't with a prostitute, I wasn't somewhere else. I was at that restaurant.

FRANCIS: I mean, the only thing I am worried about is that can he [Crick] prove that you and I actually colluded over that alibi?

ARCHER: No, you just got it wrong.

FRANCIS: I got it wrong.

ARCHER: No one can prove that. Nobody. You would need a phone conversation, you would need a private conversation. That is out of the question. You just got it wrong. I was at the restaurant and you just got it wrong. But I know how this man works and he will try and make it a big story in a national newspaper and my attitude is the following. You are down there in the West Country and you may get the press running down there and you may not.

THEY CHAT ABOUT HOLIDAYS.

ARCHER: Right, as long as we know, the truth is, I was at that restaurant so the only mistake was, it wasn't you.

FRANCIS: That's right.

ARCHER: I am very happy to tell you, it is in the restaurant book. It is in my diary.

TELEPHONE CALL FROM ARCHER TO FRANCIS AT 4.25 P.M. ON 12 NOVEMBER 1999.

ARCHER: I thought the wise thing to do was to have a chat to Mishcon. Although the man is now eighty, the brain is still like a bloody Rolls-Royce. He's taken it as a very great compliment and anyway he will bill for it [tape indistinct here] – to go in and go through the entire papers.

The following things to let you know: (1) You were never mentioned or at any time referred to in the trial or any papers connected with it. (2) I never made a statement about you – either an affidavit or statement because by the time your letter had come they had changed the date so you became an irrelevance.

He's naturally worried about how they got hold of the letter – mystified and worried – but nevertheless, he says, as long as you say nothing – they have got nothing.

After the first damning tape on 4 November, our lawyers and the editor, Phil Hall, realised we had a big story on our hands – one that would undoubtedly involve Archer appearing in court, with me as one of the key prosecution witnesses.

The News International legal manager, barrister Tom Crone, flagged up a potential problem. As I was currently on bail and charged with paying a police officer (a charge later dismissed), the defence would try to make much of this to try to discredit me in front of a jury. My colleague and friend Rob Kellaway joined me with Ted to ensure we could 'dilute' any attack on my integrity.

As our investigation came to a head, and with Michael Crick's name central to the trap I had set Archer, the last thing I needed was for this highly industrious journalist to start getting wind of what we were doing and marching all over the story and inadvertently alerting Archer to the fact that his worries were baseless. Now that Mishcon had become involved, it was more than probable he would write or ring Crick and ask him what he was playing at and try to frighten him off his non-existent investigation.

I therefore arranged for Crick to be out of the country. I arranged for someone to call the BBC *Newsnight* team and set up a bogus meeting with Michael Stacpole, one of Archer's former fixers, in Hong Kong. The message to meet Stacpole came with the promise of devastating revelations about Archer's 1987 libel trial and the condition that it should be Crick who flew out to talk to him.

In the end, Crick was nowhere to be seen on my pitch. In my version of events, it is because he was standing sweltering outside the Hong Kong Marriott, awaiting a taxi bearing Stacpole that never arrived. In Crick's version, he smelled a rat and didn't board the plane. Whatever the truth, it is always the subject of good-natured banter when we meet!

Even though our tapes were conclusive, there was a great deal of nervousness about running the story. Phil Hall was understandably cautious. To accuse a peer of the realm of attempting to pervert the course of justice in the middle of his campaign to run for the Mayor of London would be suicidal if we got it wrong. The 1987 damages pay-out of £500,000 would be at least double in 1999, as his literary and political careers had burgeoned since then. In short, it would be the end of Phil Hall and Neville Thurlbeck on Fleet Street. I was thirty-eight and would never have worked in the industry at that level again.

This perhaps explains the unorthodox approach we made to Archer before running the story. Normally, I would confront the subjects of my investigation before publication. But on this one occasion, Phil Hall and the managing editor, Stuart Kuttner, made an appointment to see Archer at his penthouse flat overlooking the Thames in central London on Saturday 20 November 1999. They were armed with 'dummies' of the following day's exposé, complete with transcripts of the damning tapes. Archer asked if he could keep them to study before considering his position.

The aim was to force Archer to realise the hopelessness of his position, admit his guilt and quit the race for Mayor of London. It worked. And we were able to run the story without the slightest fear of a disastrous libel trial with a perverse, career-ending verdict.

On 21 November 1999 we ran the story. The whole of page 1 was set aside, together with pages 2, 3, 4 and 5. Page

1 announced 'World Exclusive: Archer Quits as *News of the World* Exposes False Alibi'.

The story flew around the world. As Archer was an author of international fame, virtually every country in the civilised world ran it.

Archer's former personal assistant Angela Peppiatt then stepped forward to show Archer had lied about various critical movements during the 1987 libel trial. And on 26 September 2000, Archer was charged with perjury and perverting the course of justice during the 1987 libel trial.

Worryingly for Ted Francis, he was also charged with perverting the course of justice.

Archer was disowned by his party. Conservative leader William Hague said: 'This is the end of politics for Jeffrey Archer. I will not tolerate such behaviour in my party.' On 4 February 2000, Archer was expelled from the party for five years.

As the hugely anticipated trial loomed, Fleet Street prepared itself for what would inevitably be a series of scandalous episodes involving infidelity, mistresses, prostitutes, lies, betrayal and skulduggery. Then, just a month before the trial started, the key witness on whom the original libel trial rested, the prostitute Monica Coghlan, was killed.

On 26 April 2001, a drug addict, Gary Day, robbed a pharmacy, stole a high-powered S-type Jaguar and ploughed it into Coghlan's Ford Fiesta outside Huddersfield, West Yorkshire. Coghlan's car was catapulted over a wall and she lay in the wreckage for an hour before she was cut free. She died, aged fifty, the next day. Day admitted manslaughter and was jailed for life.

On 30 May 2001, the Old Bailey trial began. On the morning I was due to give my evidence, I walked into the large waiting area outside court number eight to await the opening of the doors. Archer sat on a bench with his barrister, who nudged him and mouthed, 'That's Thurlbeck.' Archer lowered his half-moon spectacles to the end of his nose and peered over the top to stare intensely at me for a full thirty seconds. Ever the dramatist! So I put on my specs, lowered them down my nose and peered at him over the top of them too. Ever the clown!

One of the most dramatic moments in court came when the tapes were played back. In a scene reminiscent of the Nuremberg Trials, everyone donned earphones – the defendants, lawyers, jury, judge (talking his wig off to do so) and myself. As the tapes played, everyone listened in absolute silence. Archer's distinctive clipped, staccato delivery was precise as he dissected the bogus problem I had manufactured for him.

Then came the following statement: 'Crick thinks he has got a story, of course, because he thinks you have told a lie, which he can now prove, and therefore I have told a lie because I was saying that you were at Sambuca with me when you weren't.'

The twelve men and women of the jury, who had all been sitting in hunched concentration, eased back several inches into their chairs, as if to collectively say, 'That's it. Job done.' One or two turned to look at each other. Archer was sunk.

Archer's QC, Nicholas Purnell, grilled me for three hours in the witness box but found it impossible to dispute any of our evidence.

Before sentencing Lord Archer to four years' imprisonment, the judge, Mr Justice Potts, told him: 'These charges represent as serious an offence of perjury as I have had experience of and have been able to find in the books. Sentencing you, Lord Archer, gives me no pleasure at all, I assure you. It has been an extremely distasteful case, I can tell you.'

The verdicts were unanimous on every count. Ted Francis was acquitted on the basis that he had believed his alibi was to cover for an extramarital indiscretion and not the libel trial.

Archer was found guilty of two charges of perjury and two of perverting the course of justice. The first charge was that he perverted the course of justice by asking Ted Francis to give him a false alibi. The second guilty verdict was on a charge that he perverted the course of justice by using a fake diary in the libel trial. He was found to have perjured himself in an affidavit to the High Court for the libel action. He was also found to have perjured himself on oath during the libel trial. Lord Archer, who was ordered to pay £175,000 costs within twelve months, was told by the judge he would have to serve at least half of his sentence.

There was a shout of 'yes' from the public gallery as Archer's first guilty verdict was delivered by the jury foreman. Archer showed no reaction as he stood in the dock. His wife Mary stared ahead, a crucifix hanging elegantly – and in hopeful prayer, I thought – around her neck. I felt very, very sorry for them both. There was no sense of elation. I hadn't expected this at all. All I felt was utter sadness.

It is on record that Ted Francis made £19,000 from the deal he struck with us, giving £5,000 to charity and spending the rest on a second-hand car.

On 4 September 2001, Detective Sergeant Roger Milburn, from Scotland Yard's special inquiry team, dropped me a letter. It was a letter written at the end of more than a century of successful cooperation and collaboration between the *News of the World* and the police. But it now seems of a different age.

Dear Mr Thurlbeck,

R. V. Archer & Francis
Operation Presido

On 19 July 2001, at the Central Criminal Court, Lord Archer was found guilty of Perjury and Perverting the Course of Public Justice. He was sentenced to a total of four years' imprisonment. Edward Francis was acquitted.

On behalf of the Metropolitan Police Service and myself, I would like to take this opportunity simply to thank you for your cooperation and for bearing with us so helpfully. I do hope that you have not suffered undue inconvenience. Your help was absolutely necessary to reach the verdicts we achieved. We could not have done it without you.

Yours sincerely,

Roger Milburn

The investigation won six awards. It won Scoop of the Year at the Press Awards, the What the Papers Say Awards, the Press Club Awards, the Press Ball Awards and the Campaign Magazine Press Awards, and the annual internal *News of the World* Scoop of the Year Award.

The Conservative Party leader William Hague had long been down to present the award at the British Press Awards at the Savoy, the newspaper industry Oscars. Everyone now expected him to duck out and make some pressing political engagement an excuse not to attend. But to his very great credit, he met his obligation and he carried it off with humour and style. After presenting me with the award and standing next to me as a barrage of flashbulbs exploded in front of us, he fixed his grin and whispered like a ventriloquist, 'I see. You exposed him. I had to sack him. And now we're meant to be bloody celebrating together are we?'

CHAPTER 13

RECRUITED BY THE NATIONAL CRIMINAL INTELLIGENCE SERVICE

IN FEBRUARY 1995, I was introduced to a fascinating villain called Ron Sutton who was to prove an invaluable contact for many years to come. Ron mixed with a wide cross-section of crooks and selected the ones he didn't like to expose in the *News of the World*. An immensely likeable rough diamond with a gift for easy patter, he could worm his way into a gangleader's trust within minutes. And when the going got tough, he could talk – or punch – his way out of a shark's mouth.

He stood barely 5ft 5in. tall but was stocky and with beetling eyebrows that met in the middle. His overly long ears carried a slight deformity that gave him an extra flap of skin at the top and lobes that were fastened to the side of his head.

Imagine a heavy from a 1940s Ealing comedy and you have Ron Sutton. Or almost. As with most villains, there is a dark side, and Ron's was a violent one. Coming home one afternoon, he found his girlfriend in bed with another man and beat him senseless with the nearest thing to hand, which happened to be a cricket bat. He was sentenced to five years in prison and served every bit of it with not so much as a day off for good behaviour, such was his aggression to warders and hostility to any authority figure who crossed his path.

Despite this, he had a roguish charm, almost like the Lovejoy TV character played by Ian McShane. The combination made Ron trusted, feared and liked by villains, all at the same time. Coupled with his strong news sense and the courage of a lion, he was going to be gold dust to us.

We got off to a flying start. We were an odd couple to look at. He the swarthy working-class villain, me the clean-cut middle-class ... well, what exactly? Ron was going to have to introduce me to gangs so I could infiltrate them and try to get the proof we needed to expose them. Dressing down, growing a beard and becoming a coarse ruffian was one option. But villains are good at spotting someone who isn't one of them. I opted to play to my own characteristics and bolt on a few unsavoury bits. So I remained middle class, I remained clean shaven, I still parted my hair and I even wore a blazer or a tweed jacket. I was still 'Neville', too. Undercover operatives will always tell you, while you should change your surname, never change your Christian name. Your associates will eventually slip up and blurt out your real name on a job. And you can never discount the possibility of someone who knows you bumping into you when you are with a villain and shouting, 'Hey, Nev, how are you?'

I devised a cover story to fit this image. I had been a captain in the army who had been court-martialled for taking and dealing cocaine. Disgraced and unable to find work, I was now earning a living dealing drugs/selling counterfeit money/peddling pornography – whatever I needed to pretend in order to gain the trust of the gang. Luckily, it worked every time and I was never rumbled, threatened or attacked. The image I portrayed was so different to undercover police tactics (they always assume the role of rough, coarse villain), no one ever even suspected me. I was hiding in plain view.

Within days of meeting Ron, we had exposed two paedophiles. And as the weeks went by, the page leads and two-page spreads mounted as we infiltrated gangs who were peddling guns, drugs or counterfeit money. Ron's productivity mounted and there came a point where I was driving up to his 'manor' in Hinckley, Leicestershire every week, setting up base at the Millers Hotel in the hamlet of Sibson and finding a target for the week to work on. By the end of 1995, I had spent nine months away from home with him.

Sometimes working undercover was simply not possible and a 'surrogate' undercover operative would have to be deployed – one who could be guided by me by 'remote control'. A typical example involved a gang of Metropolitan Police officers who were selling hard drugs, but only to their trusted customers. The tipster in this case was a fellow police officer and he was the only person able to infiltrate their conspiracy, tape it and give it to me to expose in the paper (he was later disciplined for doing so).

I was so invisible on this undercover job, when the police officers appeared in court to plead guilty, I stood next to them in the court waiting area as a mere observer as they chatted among themselves and their wives. One complained loudly, 'Who the hell is this Neville Thurlbeck, anyway? Has anyone even seen the bugger?' He was wearing a Barbour coat and I quietly slipped my business card into his pocket, which I imagine would have rather spooked him when he fished it out later.

In April 1995, Ron came up with another drug story. But this one was to have major implications for the rest of my career. He claimed he could introduce me to the country's only importer of a deadly drug called Phencyclidine, known as PCP or angel dust on the street.

The drug destroys all reason and instils a lunatic illusion of power, and it had caused mayhem in the USA. One young mum stabbed her seven-year-old daughter thirty-five times. In New York, a student had gouged his own eyes out and another pulled his own teeth out with pliers. Police in California had developed special nets that they used for trapping crazed users.

The paranoia about this devastating drug reaching British shores consumed our law enforcement agencies behind the scenes. The potential for mass outbreaks of mindless and brutal violence had so concerned them that MI5 had become involved in 1993. At the end of 1994, the National Criminal Intelligence Service (now part of the Serious Organised Crime Agency) got involved too. But no hard evidence of its existence could be found.

But David and Anne Lodde, a husband-and-wife drug dealing team, were on the verge of flooding the market with a big consignment from Holland. But to get to them, I had to go through a chain. Ron introduced me to two small-time cannabis dealers who knew someone who knew the Loddes. The Loddes were three introductions away from me. But after a few meetings, I progressed up the chain and managed to get an invitation to a 'fetish party' the Loddes were due to attend at Club UK in Wandsworth, south-west London.

The club was packed with people displaying the nature of their fetish. Men were being led around the floor on their hands and knees at the end of dog leads by stern-looking women in high-heeled boots, basques and stockings. Others were chained up inside small cages wearing leather gimp masks. Some men paraded around dressed as babies, complete with nappy and dummy. Ecstasy tablets were being popped left, right and centre, and techno music boomed through the high-wattage speakers, making conversation impossible. In dark corners, couples graduated from displaying their fetishes to performing them on each other.

In order to blend in with this scene of manic debauchery, my contact had provided me with a costume to help me blend in with all the high jinks. The costume of black leather trousers, jackboots and riding crop seemed to me to miss the point a little. I wouldn't have minded being a Nazi, a biker or a horseman. But the resulting ensemble rather diluted the effect of all three. Curious girls kept asking me, 'What have you come as?' My reply could never be heard over the din, so I explained, 'I'm Stan Laurel – during his leather phase' to all of them. This somehow seemed to do the trick as they all nodded approvingly, some of them even pouting their appreciation at my 'sexual deviancy'. No one at a fetish party likes to admit to sexual naïveté!

At the party, in order to gain the trust of the Loddes, I had to buy a small quantity of ecstasy and amphetamines ('speed') to prove my credentials. Buying drugs on jobs was a regular occurrence for me by now and to avoid falling foul of the law I would fax my intention to do so to a trusted, Home Office-approved chemist in Acton, who would analyse them for me afterwards. I was never tempted to sample any of them, however fashionable it was at the time. I had tried one line of cocaine at university in 1982 and the effect had been so pleasurable I had vowed never to try it again, realising I would become hooked very easily. And I have stuck to that decision with regard to all illegal drugs since. Beer and cigarettes were the vices of my youth. Even the cigarettes have long gone now.

David Lodde was a fearsome-looking man of around 6ft 4in., a body-builder and a wall of muscle. He had thick, rubbery lips and a deep, growling south London accent. His wife, Anne, was a slightly-built, cockney sparrow type.

The introduction went well. The contacts introduced me as 'Neville', the dodgy army captain who flogged drugs. Lodde flogged his little package to me and before leaving, I told him to get in touch with me if he could get hold of something 'a bit different and extremely heavy'. Lodde saw the door opening for a lucrative transaction involving his PCP. He said: 'PCP is the stuff. I call them brain-fuckers. They're really mean. I can get as much as you want.' He said he would sell me a sample for £15 a tablet with more to follow. He also offered to sell 1,000 ecstasy tablets at £7 each and we arranged to meet a day later at a café in Whipps Cross Road, Leytonstone.

The following day, Lodde arrived at the café in the customary black BMW and handed over two angel dust tablets and two pieces of blotting paper soaked in the lethal chemical. I was wired up to capture the drugs sales patter that followed. He said, 'People who use this are usually out of their heads on other stuff.' He laughed at this. Then added, 'Make sure you don't do more than half a tablet. You can lose your marbles. You know when you do too much acid? Well, it's the same, but worse. The good thing is, if you imagine you are in a pile of female bodies, you will feel them, know what I mean?

'There are not many tablets but the papers are in infinite supply. But you can get into a lot of trouble. These are very, very naughty things. That's why I am so, so careful when I sell them to anybody.'

As the transaction took place, sitting in a blacked-out surveillance van 20 yards away was Brian Roberts, one of the best photographers at the *News of the World*. Using a long lens, he captured the exact moment the drugs were handed over. The picture showed a hulking, tattooed, streetwise drug dealer handing over one of the most lethal drugs ever found on these shores – to a clean-cut young chap wearing a blazer and chinos. It was the biggest test of the rogue army captain persona so far, and it had worked.

Lodde had promised me as much of the drug as I'd wanted and after it was analysed and proven to be the feared PCP, I brought in the police. One of my contacts was DC Dick Farmer, who had been seconded to the National Criminal Intelligence Service (NCIS), which was also a bridging point between Special Branch and the domestic security service MI5. Dick and his colleagues came to our Wapping HQ and we formed a plan to catch the Loddes red handed. But one or two tablets wasn't enough. A small amount would only get him a slap on the wrist. And if Lodde was the major dealer we believed he was, the police wanted him off the streets for a long time.

We decided to leave the Loddes alone for a week or two to let them relax a little. They were already on the end of the hook, but to try to reel them in too quickly might have made them suspicious. I called them to say I couldn't get the cash together straight away and I would be in touch a week or two later – a shortage of cash being the very last thing that would have troubled an undercover policeman, had the Loddes begun to suspect me of being one.

A fortnight later, I called him on the mobile and struck a deal. A hundred and fifty tablets for £1,350. The deal to take place in a field near Leytonstone the following day. Immediately after, the Loddes were to be arrested by plain-clothes police hiding in bushes. The police would be armed. And there would be eight of them.

I was warned of the potential dangers. Lodde could be armed. If he pulled out a gun or a knife, they would open fire. If he suspected I was an undercover policeman, he might shoot me first. To minimise the potential of a bloodbath, they decided to 'arrest' me at the same time and release me once the Loddes were handcuffed and in the back of a police van.

At the appointed hour, I stood in the middle of a small field with the Nagra tape recorder strapped to my back and silently whirring away. The Loddes pulled up in their black BMW and started walking towards me. I really wanted the thing over and done with as quickly as possible, as I was feeling more than a little anxious. Luckily, one of the few useful things I took away from university was the ability to control my nerves. Standing on a stage in front of 800 people with 1,000 lines of seventeenth-century dialogue to deliver and with no prompt (by the early '80s, prompts were frowned on as 'too am-dram') could be potentially paralysing to a twenty-year-old. So I did the deep-breathing routine and slowly brought my heart rate down, falling into the role of the disgraced army captain. Suddenly, I wasn't Neville Thurlbeck, worried about it all ending rather dismally in a hail of bullets. I was Neville, playing a role and anxious that he didn't miss his cue or bump into the furniture!

The cue on this occasion was to remove my hat when the drug deal had 'gone down'. The moment I had possession of the drugs and had handed over the cash, I removed my trilby, which was the signal for the police to move in.

I had expected mayhem to break out. But slowly, five very ordinary-looking middle-aged men, all dressed like dads on a Saturday afternoon stroll, appeared from separate points of the compass and began closing in on us. No guns were drawn. Lodde remained oblivious to what was about to happen as he stuffed the wad of cash into his jeans pocket.

The smallest of the officers, a man in his mid-fifties and about 5ft 7in. tall (a good 9 inches and 6 stone lighter than his quarry), placed his hand on Lodde's left arm and quietly told him he was under arrest. Another two officers calmly took his other arm and forced him onto the ground and onto his stomach, cuffing his hands behind his back. Two other officers performed the same task on me. Lodde's wife bolted but was apprehended and arrested a hundred yards away. The two were loaded into a police van and taken down to the station. When the van was out of sight, my handcuffs were unlocked.

The officers involved didn't even break into a sweat. But it was their calmness that prevented panic and bloodshed. Their guns remained holstered and a very dangerous man was seized with just a few quiet words from a middle-aged man. Their bravery and professionalism were exemplary. This very British type of arrest, often in the face of mortal danger, is carried out by every force in the British Isles every day. We are wise to remember this as we are wont to criticise the police when their occasional shortcomings come to light.

In December 1996, the couple pleaded guilty at Snaresbrook Crown Court, London, to supplying drugs. Lodde was sentenced to five years in prison and his wife three and a half years. Sentencing them, Judge David Radford said, 'Clearly, the offences on this indictment are so serious that only an immediate custodial sentence can be justified.'

Speaking outside court, DC Chris Jelley, who led the investigation, was kind enough to say: 'It is a number of years since PCP has been seized in this country and this is the largest amount seized, ever. Without Mr Thurlbeck, we wouldn't have convicted these two people for drug dealing.'

But it was the quieter NCIS that had been following the matter with the greatest interest. After the arrests, their spokesman said, 'The *News of the World* has done a great public service. Congratulations on a first-class piece of undercover work.'

And it was the undercover work that had interested them most. Within a matter of days, they requested a further meeting with me and I suggested an office at our old Wapping HQ. Two men in bland suits arrived one Tuesday morning in June 1995 to discuss 'how we can help each other'. The meeting began with a lot of questions about my background and then moved on to the nature of my contacts in the underworld.

Of particular interest to them was the number of investigations I discarded as being of no interest. To a Sunday tabloid, a schoolteacher selling a joint of cannabis is more interesting than a Yardie selling a kilo of heroin, simply because, well, to put it bluntly, that's what Yardies do. It's what can be termed a 'bear shits in the woods' story. We were, after all, a newspaper, not a law enforcement agency. To 'get into' a Yardie gang would take months of planning and would result in a story of little or no interest to the readers.

The following week, I was invited out for a drink with an NCIS officer, where he explained that his organisation wanted to recruit me, part-time, as an undercover operative. Getting into gangs was one of the hardest parts of any operation and they seemed to appreciate the methods I had used.

I explained that this was out of the question as I was working between sixty and eighty hours a week for the paper and my working week could never be planned more than a day or so ahead. I couldn't be relied upon.

A second suggestion was offered. Would I be prepared to be a paid informant? I didn't like the idea of this either, as this arrangement would be open to a variety of interpretations, not least of which could be the suspicion of my editor that I was deliberately depriving my paper of stories by selling them to the police.

In the end, we opted for a third option. I would be what

NCIS termed a 'registered confidential source'. No money would change hands. I would provide them with leads on stories we had deemed beyond our scope or interest involving drug smuggling, gun-running and sex crimes. If I had already infiltrated a criminal organisation and decided to bale out, I would slowly introduce one of their men. In return, they would provide me with back-up assistance. This largely involved supplying me with criminal record checks on people I was investigating to see if they had 'form' for whatever crime I was investigating them for. And they would help me by providing addresses from the registration numbers of vehicles I was following. This in turn would lead to the real identity of a criminal I was pursuing. All very helpful indeed to a tabloid journalist – and an arrangement that will perhaps shock you a little now in this post-Leveson era of non-cooperation between the press and the police.

By 1995, I was an NCIS operative, code-named 'Agent George' with the registration number 251. The relationship between the press and the police has never been closer than this. And, in the coming months and years, this arrangement would take me to the very heart of the security services.

CHAPTER 14

MI5

FOR THE NEXT few years, my relationship with NCIS grew quite close, to the extent that I was speaking to them up to three or four times a week. Much of the intelligence I was able to provide concerned serious organised crime involving the movement of guns, drugs or money, or occasionally a paedophile gang if I had tried and failed to infiltrate them.

The help I received in return was so valuable I was able to expose numerous criminal or nefarious enterprises. In 1996, I was promoted to crime reporter and then to chief crime reporter in 1998. I spent many months of the year away from home, infiltrating gangs and mixing with some pretty unsavoury types. But thanks to my NCIS contacts, my job was made a whole lot easier.

This meant I could corroborate the information being fed to me or discover a particular criminal's past modus operandi, his background, associates, addresses and even the pubs he drank in or car he drove. It also meant that, by knowing some of his back story, I could adapt mine to create a background which at some point interlocked plausibly with his, and thereby gain his trust. This backstory typically included shared knowledge of a dead associate or his 'manor'.

All Fleet Street crime reporters belong to an organisation called the Crime Reporters Association. It's a very useful body to belong to, as it is trusted by the official police media channels, which will often provide off-the-record briefings on big crime stories to the association's members. Needless to say, I never joined. Even on Fleet Street, I was for ever destined to be an outsider, preferring to do things my own way, for better or for worse. My unofficial contacts at NCIS provided me with everything I needed and I had no wish to belong to a club that might expect me to share anything I had found off my own bat. I'm a bit tightly wrapped in that way, I'm afraid.

As ever, going it alone on Fleet Street is a risky strategy. If everyone on Fleet Street got the inside steer on a major crime story and I didn't, it could be career-ending. Fortunately, it never happened. I can honestly say I was never scooped by anyone. And in 1999, I was nominated for my second award at the British Press Awards for Specialist Reporter of the Year for a string of crime exclusives.

Occasionally, I unearthed intelligence which had national security implications, and from the mid-1990s onwards, I was in contact with MI5, a relationship that was to continue on and off for the next sixteen years.

MI5, with its history of intrigue, espionage and mystery, is often seen as a glamorous enterprise. In fact, it is simply a gigantic information-gathering bureau. Going up in one of the lifts for the first time at Thames House, its imposing HQ on the embankment, I shared my journey not with sharp-suited James Bond types but with two ladies wearing the Muslim veil. Another chap was clearly of Middle Eastern origin. Another looked like a scruffy university student with a torn rucksack slung over his shoulder. He seemed like a black African. Of course, when you think about it, it's obvious that if you are going to infiltrate an extremist Muslim sect it is better to be a black Muslim than to look like a white, university-educated James Bond.

Much of the work at MI5 is very dull indeed. Gathering information on people doesn't mean shadowing them unseen as they travel to exotic climes, although this is very occasionally the case. The vast majority of surveillance work is carried out digitally. This effectively means finding out who is communicating with whom and what they are saying – normally on email, mobile phones or from fixed landlines or 'bugs' designed to eavesdrop. Vast amounts of collated data from phone companies, email servers and various eavesdropping sources will have to be collated, sifted for relevance, analysed and then pushed up the chain to a higher command to interpret or action. It can be mind-numbingly dull. The people who carry out these assignments are surprisingly ordinary, though extremely bright. Many of them are casually dressed to the point of being scruffy. Most are tieless and carry rucksacks rather than briefcases. They tend to be reserved and with well-balanced egos. They find it easy not to talk about themselves. Most of all, they are diligent, intelligent and extremely methodical. They are also very poorly paid for the work they do. Towards the end of my career at the *News of the World*, I had to deal with someone very senior, who reported directly to the assistant director general, and he informed me that I was paid more than his boss, which was extremely humbling.

If there was ever a chap to explode the mythical stereotype of the dashing James Bond, it was this fellow, with his off-the-peg high-street suit and the sort of comedy socks you might get for Christmas, with a Bart Simpson motif. He was also very warm and witty, with a delivery not unlike the comedian Michael McIntyre. His carefree attitude belied the fact that he'd spent most of his career working with grim determination and astonishing success on counterterrorism matters, especially the threat posed by the IRA. To his neighbours, he worked in the pensions department at the Home Office. To his colleagues, he was the very important man on the top floor of Thames House with an office overlooking the river.

There are several branches within MI5, requiring different disciplines from various personality types. But if one thing marks them out, it is their blandness. Near the bottom of the chain are surveillance officers or 'watchers', who follow their targets on foot or in vehicles. Some are drawn from the quieter parts of the police force or from the military. But others are selected because of their race, religion and colour. They are just as likely to be an Ahmed as a James. Women are also well represented.

This is about the nearest you'd get to a TV or film 'spook' and it's a highly skilled and difficult job. No matter how much preparation, planning, intelligence-gathering or manpower has been put into a job, a surveillance convoy can always come unstuck at a busy set of traffic lights.

Unlike my work with NCIS, my relationship with the domestic security service was not symbiotic and the information highway was strictly a one-way street. There were numerous conversations about joining their staff, but financial commitments made it impossible to take a drastic salary cut. By now I had acquired an eye-watering mortgage on a house in Esher, Surrey, and private school fees. And I'd also witnessed first-hand the drudgery of a lot of their work. Besides, I'm not altogether sure I am suited to a life of espionage. A spy must keep the astonishing facts he uncovers a secret, sometimes for the rest of his life. As a tabloid journalist, my default instinct is to write the story in every lurid detail and yell, 'Extra! Extra! Read all about it!' from the nearest street corner.

My relationship with NCIS and MI5 did provide me with many friendships, some of which endure to this day. It's very hard to gain the trust of someone in the security services, but once you do, the bond of trust is extremely strong and lifelong friendships are born.

One of my best friendships followed my introduction to a man called Rab Wood, an SAS veteran and MI6 operative. I first met Rab in the 1980s, when I was in my early twenties and he a little older. Rab was instructing me how to use a Browning 9mm pistol.

Guns have never interested me and I was more curious to find out if he could, unarmed, disarm a person with a gun.

Usual Rab nonchalance and non-committal noises ensued. Foolishly, I persisted. Eventually he relented. 'OK, here's the gun. It's not loaded but I want you to listen very carefully. Press the gun into the small of my back, shout, "Hands up!" and pull the trigger, and I'll show you.'

At this point, I have to confess, I was more than a little nervous. If truth be told, I started back-peddling on the whole idea. 'No, no … just talk me through it, man!' – that sort of thing. Rab was having none of it. I'd nagged him into it, he was going to show me and there was no going back.

I took the Browning, placed it in the small of his back, shouted, 'Hands up!' and pulled, or at least tried to pull, the trigger.

In an instant, I was stunned and face down on the floor with my gun hand behind my back as Rab wrenched it from my grasp. Seeing me sprawled on the floor, half concussed, he gently helped me back to my feet, gave me a big hug, kissed me on the cheek, threw his head back and roared with laughter.

After making sure I was OK, he took me through the whole procedure – which had lasted barely two seconds – in slow motion.

As I had pressed the Browning into the small of his back,

Rab had forced his body onto the muzzle of the pistol, causing the 'barrel to slide' mechanism to jam. So when I pulled the trigger, it jammed too. This is when Rab swung his left arm behind him and landed a very, very strong blow to the left side of my jaw with his elbow.

I was stunned to the point of starting to fall to the floor. Rab spun round, grabbed my pistol hand and pushed me to the floor face down with my pistol hand behind my back before disarming me.

I was confounded. Rab was concerned to make sure he hadn't broken my jaw, moving it from side to side and asking, 'Can you feel anything grinding?'

After declaring myself fit, I casually mentioned it had been a very good job indeed that that gun wasn't loaded. Rab looked at me, grinned that famous slightly jagged grin of his, pointed the gun into the air and pulled the trigger.

It was.

Drinking with Rab in the Special Forces Club in Knightsbridge, quite possibly the most exclusive club in the world, showed the esteem in which he was held in this close-knit community as he mingled with veterans from the Second World War Special Operations Executive and MI6 operatives with equal familiarity. It was here that he did me the honour of nicknaming me 'Low Level Neville', explaining to members that my USP was an ability to remain unseen and undetected. The expression 'low level' was derived from his military speak for a person who avoids detection as a plane does (or did), by flying extremely low to avoid being picked up by radar. Some people may also think it most appropriate for a red-top tabloid journalist!

Sadly, Rab was killed in Bulawayo, Zimbabwe, where he owned a diamond mine, in March 2012, in circumstances which have yet to be fully explained. He was fifty-four. The news came like a bolt out of the blue just a few minutes after I'd arrived at the wedding of my friend Eben Black. It's impossible to write much about Rab without incurring a D-notice. But above all else, he was a courageous, outrageous, daring, bold, kind, affectionate, loving, loyal chum. He was one of the toughest men I've met, and yet quite sensitive. At one of our last meetings, during a lunch at our home, he shed tears at the memory of colleagues who had been killed in previous operations.

The last time I saw him was in August 2011, when the phone-hacking storm was raging around the *News of the World*. He invited me out for a drink, conscious of the difficulties I was facing, despite what I later learned were increasing dangers and pressures he was facing himself. As we shook hands and parted in Sloane Square, he simply smiled and said, 'Remember, if there is anything you need, just call me.'

His funeral in Woking in April 2012 was attended by many from the security services, several of whom I hadn't seen for many years. Afterwards, at the bar of the Artists Rifles Clubhouse in Bisley, Surrey, long-lost faces sauntered over to say hello, almost all of them beginning, 'Hi, Low Level!'

CHAPTER 15

ON TRIAL

THE RELATIONSHIP BETWEEN the press and the police and security services was a fraught one even in the 1990s. People outside the industry often assumed my exposure of criminals would make me the policeman's best friend. But when you expose a criminal on the turf of a particular constabulary, resentment can set in. Somewhere down the line, a detective will be asked by his boss why the *News of the World* knew about this or that drug dealer and he did not. As a result, detectives could be tetchy when they were taking statements from me or receiving tapes. For this reason, I was always happier dealing with NCIS, who were always grateful for my help.

But, eventually, someone proved pretty determined to put a stop to my activities. My main contact at NCIS was DC Dick Farmer and an anonymous caller rang his parent force, Hertfordshire Constabulary, alleging Dick was receiving cash from me for performing checks on the Police National Computer (PNC). The arrangement, had it been true, would have been illegal under the 1906 Prevention of Corruption Act and punishable with a lengthy prison sentence for both of us.

The police launched Operation Guatemala, involving sixty police officers investigating and tracking our every movement. At one stage, we later learned, there were more police trying to prove the unfounded allegation that I was paying a few pounds to a copper than there were trying to catch the murderer of Jill Dando.

I also later learned from our contacts at BT that my home phone line had been tapped for many months – after being approved by the Home Secretary Jack Straw.

It soon became clear to us that we were being followed. Every time we met, people would hang around us implausibly. Once, on the Underground, I stepped onto a carriage, followed closely by two familiar faces. As the sliding doors began to shut, I quickly stepped back off. One of the followers made the mistake of panicking and, in a reflex reaction, instinctively tried to follow me off. He retreated swiftly as the doors jammed against him and his colleague gave him a look of thunder as he compromised their undercover operation. I raised my hat to them as the train sped off, confirming to them that he had. It was a moment that could have graced any 1930s Alfred Hitchcock movie and was slightly comical.

I still had no idea why I was being followed. It seemed too professional an operation to be the work of villains, and any number of theories presented themselves. In those days, when mobile phone batteries and signals were poor, I carried a paging device so my news desk could reach me at a moment's notice. I was aware the police would clone the pagers of suspects in order to keep tabs on their messages. So I sent myself a series of pager messages, purporting to come from Dick, arranging to meet me at various different pubs on certain days and times. At these 'meetings', I would arrive alone and observe the 'customers' in the bar. After a few days, I spotted at least two men who had been at another (bogus) arranged meeting. And given that both pubs were 12 miles apart – one the Olde Bell in Fleet Street and the other the Fox and Grapes in Wimbledon village – there were two obvious conclusions. Firstly, the police were on my tail. Secondly, it was my relationship with Dick that was exciting their suspicions.

A few weeks later, Dick noticed a small screw had appeared in the dashboard of his unmarked Ford Mondeo, which NCIS had given to him for his personal and business use. He unscrewed it and a tracking device fell out, indicating it had been installed by his bosses to keep track of his movements. He walked straight in to see his commanding officer. Time had been called on their massive surveillance operation and they arrested Dick on the spot, on suspicion of taking bribes from a journalist.

Several weeks later, I took my car to be serviced at the local Mercedes dealer. When I returned to collect it, as I drove out of the forecourt, the heating apparatus inexplicably fell down through the dashboard. The bashful-looking mechanics hastily reassembled it, offering no explanation as to how it had happened. I later learned from a very senior police source it was because the police had installed a tracking device in my car, behind the heating unit. The car was just a year old and they figured I would have it serviced by the local Mercedes dealer in order not to invalidate the warranty. They had contacted the dealer and asked him to tip them off the next time my car was booked in for a service. And when it duly arrived, in went the police with their tracking device. This explained how the undercover surveillance team always turned up at our meetings. The tracking device warned them on a computer every time our cars looked like converging on one another and off they shot.

Later, after Dick's arrest and with bail conditions preventing him from seeing me, they had no further use for the tracking device in my car. So when it went in for the next service, out came the dashboard, the heating apparatus and the tracker. Except this time, the job was botched. Out fell the heater!

It was only a matter of time before the police would want to question me, but it was six long months before they put in their request to do so.

The request came in the form of a loud knock on my front door at 7.20 a.m. on 20 October 1998. I answered the door, covered in shaving cream. Outside there were three unmarked police cars and seven plain-clothes detectives. One of them announced in a loud voice that he was arresting me on suspicion of paying a police officer and wanted entry to my home. I asked to see a search warrant and he told me he didn't need one and barged straight past into the hall, followed by his six colleagues.

First of all, they explained, they wanted to search the house. I explained that my wife was in bed feeding our three-month-old daughter and told them to reduce the volume at which they were barking at me and stamping around the house. I picked up the phone and told them I was calling the office to arrange a lawyer immediately. The lead officer shouted: 'You can't do that!' I ignored him and dialled David Rigby, the number three on the news desk at the time.

I got straight to the point in case they tried to snatch the phone from me. 'David, get me a lawyer pronto. I've seven cops in the hallway and they are going to search the house.'

I went upstairs to dress, followed by a police officer, while his six colleagues charged around the house shouting and trying to look and sound assertive. Drawers were pulled out and cupboards searched. I did my best to reassure my wife before I was led out of the front door and into one of the cars, where I was sandwiched in the back between two officers. As the convoy sped off towards Hatfield Police Station in Hertfordshire, I asked why they had come mob-handed. 'In case you didn't comply with our need for a search,' came the reply. I wondered if they thought I was going to try to blast my way out!

An image flashed through my mind of some long-forgotten British B movie where the villain (probably Dirk Bogarde or Dickie Attenborough) aims his revolver and, with beads of cold sweat on his upper lip, announces grimly, 'You'll never take me alive, copper.'

My chuckle was just audible because one of the 'assertive' officers asked roughly, 'What's there to laugh at?'

'You,' I replied. 'And the comedy of this badly acted pantomime. Relax and stop pretending to be assertive and you might improve your chances of success.' They didn't seem to like this and for the rest of the ninety-minute journey, we sat in silence.

At Hatfield, I was shown to a filthy cell. The door was clashed shut and I sat on a bench covered by a plastic cushion. In the corner, a dirty lavatory was perched in full view of the door and observation hatch. A small window let in some watery light through toughened, translucent glass several inches thick. After an hour, the door opened and I was invited to a room to have my fingerprints taken and mouth swabs for DNA tests. My police mugshot was taken and I was led back to the cell to await the arrival of my lawyer, Henri Brandman.

When Henri arrived, we agreed to let the police ask as many questions as they wished. But we would not be commenting. It was up to them to make their case and we would take a view later as to whether we wanted to add anything. I certainly wasn't going to give them anything that would compromise my contact Dick Farmer and land him with a serious disciplinary.

I was thirty-seven years old, with a large mortgage and two daughters, one aged five and another three months. Suddenly I was facing the prospect of jail and ruin. I was driven home after hours of questioning and felt pretty desolate. That evening

I drank the contents of an unopened bottle of cognac that had been sitting in the drinks cabinet for years. Slowly, over the course of the evening as I pondered my uncertain future, the cognac vanished. Drinking a bottle of spirits is something I had never done before and have never done since. And, oddly, I went to bed sober.

The following day, I returned to work. Phil Hall, the editor, kindly invited me to take as much time off as I needed. Instead, I decided to carry on working. I'd never taken a day's sick leave in my life, like my father and his father too. No male Thurlbeck had taken a day off work since the First World War and I wasn't going to be the first. It was to be business as usual.

I'm glad I carried on, as it was to prove a very productive time for me, landing the Jeffrey Archer story and numerous awards and nominations for undercover work.

It took them until December 1999 – fourteen months later – to charge both myself and Dick with corruption, and the trial didn't take place until the summer of 2000, meaning I had spent twenty-one months on police bail being investigated.

The downside to this was the enormous stress it placed on my family, old and young alike. My then five-year-old daughter was and still is a very perceptive creature. During one of my prolonged periods of silent anxiety, she asked: 'Daddy, have you got something inside your head?' My mother-in-law sadly died in April 1999 and as she lay on her deathbed, I tried to alleviate her anxiety by pretending the charges had been dropped. These are the untold consequences of police

investigations into journalists. As I write, I face yet another
uncertain future as a possible jail sentence looms as a consequence of the work I carried out with the full knowledge,
encouragement and acceptance of News UK. I accept those
consequences. But I cannot forgive the company for the pain
it has caused my family through its reckless disregard.

The pressure on Dick had been colossal. He suffered a severe
nervous breakdown and arrived in the dock a husk of a man.

The trial, when it came, was at Luton Crown Court and
was presided over by a High Court judge. Mr Justice Stuart
McKinnon. After two weeks of hearing the prosecution's case,
it was clearly going nowhere. Sometimes you can spot when
a jury is sceptical of the charges and such a moment came
after about a week.

I had written a story about a cab driver with convictions
for violent rape, warning women not to enter his cab, with
pictures of a great hulking brute illustrating it. Dick had provided me with the evidence of his horrific crimes from the
police national computer.

Roy Amlott QC was defending me, and Bob Marshall-
Andrews QC was defending Dick. Marshall-Andrews rose
to his feet to cross-examine the main police witness, DCI
Graham Hunt, who had led the investigation.

MARSHALL-ANDREWS: Would you agree with me that this
article was very much in the public interest?
DCI HUNT: No.

MARSHALL-ANDREWS: Were you aware that this man who Thurlbeck was warning about later went on to work for another taxi firm?

DCI HUNT: No.

MARSHALL-ANDREWS: Then you won't be aware that he went on to kidnap one of his fares, rape her, murder her, cut up her body and dump it in some bushes in Bisley, Surrey?

DCI HUNT: No.

MARSHALL-ANDREWS: Now that you do know, do you now think that this important article was in the public interest?

DCI HUNT: No.

At this point there was a loud groan from the twelve men and women on the jury. With one word, he had lost them.

Soon after, the judge called a halt and ordered the jury to acquit us both, as there was no evidence of any money changing hands and therefore no corruption.

Mr Justice Stuart McKinnon said:

> There was a legitimate and appropriate relationship which can be explained without any suggestion of corruption. A symbiotic one – a two-way relationship with information passed both ways.
>
> Mr Thurlbeck undoubtedly supplied information to Mr Farmer which was of interest to the police. In return for which Mr Farmer provided to Mr Thurlbeck not confidential or sensitive information, but information principally

about criminals' previous convictions, which he obtained
from the Police National Computer.

We were free to go. I rang my wife, who cried with relief,
I enjoyed a scotch and soda with my legal team and then I
headed back to the office.

On my return, the new editor, Rebekah Wade (now Brooks),
had arranged a small party for me in her office. Among the
assembled guests waiting to welcome me back with a glass of
champagne were the company's chief executive officer Les Hinton, the *News of the World*'s managing editor Stuart Kuttner,
the deputy editor Bob Bird, and numerous executives. Stuart
had assured me after my arrest that my job was safe whatever
the outcome, even if it had resulted in me being jailed. At the
party, he reminded me of that reassurance and Les confirmed
that he had sanctioned it. Les had also sanctioned the cost of
my defence, which was £360,000 – a colossal sum not only in
those days but even now.

In those days, News International (now known as News
UK), was incredibly protective of its staff and would stand by
them through thick and thin if they deserved it. Les Hinton
was a Murdoch man through and through, a man Murdoch
would later famously say he would 'trust with his life'. He presided over News International with his forceful, dynamic vision
but also with a lightness of touch and, as a former *Sun* journalist of renown, he commanded universal respect throughout
the company. He was impressed that, despite the pressure of

the police investigation, I had pulled off the Archer scoop, and his warm words of praise and encouragement were gratefully received by this humble crime reporter.

As the small gathering dispersed, Rebekah offered me time off to recover from the whole episode but, once again, I thanked her and declined, in order to preserve the family working record. (It should be noted as this point, however, that while no male Thurlbeck has taken a day off since the First World War, not one of them has lived long enough to claim his state pension!)

I returned to my desk to make a few calls. It was business as usual.

But under Rebekah's new editorship and then that of her successor, Andy Coulson, my life on the *News of the World* would become dramatic, colourful, entertaining and extremely demanding. It would see the fortunes of the paper alter dramatically – and mine with them.

CHAPTER 16

NEWS EDITOR

REBEKAH FORMED A small investigations unit, headed by Greg Miskiw, with me as the investigations news editor, Greg's number two. It also consisted of Mazher Mahmood – the 'fake sheikh' – and a couple of others. And in the following twelve months, we managed to break thirteen splashes: exactly 25 per cent of the annual total of fifty-two splashes, with about 10 per cent of the newspaper staff. The unit was so successful that just a year after its formation, in June 2001, Greg was promoted to head up the news desk as assistant editor (news) with me as his number two, this time as news editor.

Being the news editor of the biggest newspaper in the English-speaking world is not without its pressures! I rose each day at 5.30 a.m., put on my gym kit, picked up my suit and clothes and drove through the empty morning streets from Esher to Wapping. After a session in the company gym, a shower and a quick breakfast, I was at my desk and reading the papers by 7.30 a.m. And there I frequently remained until 8 p.m., 9 p.m. and then midnight as the week progressed towards deadline.

I had a team of around thirty reporters and the services of scores of freelances throughout Britain and abroad, and more than a million pounds to spend each year. There was no excuse for failing to deliver stories and no excuse for being beaten by the opposition. Rebekah and Andy never tolerated coming second and I didn't expect them to. Neither did I.

The one time Andy thought I had messed up on the desk and missed something, the explosion was terrific. I was in charge of the desk when the *Columbia* space shuttle broke up on re-entry, killing all seven on board on 1 February 2003. A piece of Reuters copy came on the wire around 10 p.m., stating that the cause of the disaster was thought to be a damaged left wing. My deputy, David Jarvis, flagged it up to me. I told him to push it quickly to the back bench, where the sub-editors sift and sort urgent stories on a Saturday night, and to mark it up as 'urgent', which he did. It was missed. So we failed to carry the major development in the story. Everyone else in Fleet Street had it.

When Andy telephoned me at home at 2 a.m. to complain, he needn't have bothered. I'd have heard him if he'd just shouted out of his window 20 miles away! No excuses were accepted. I don't think I got a word in edgeways to try to even mount a defence. Such episodes are common on Fleet Street, especially between editors and news editors. There is the constant shout for, 'more, more, more' from the editor. Along with, 'Why has this paper got it and not us?', 'Where are the big stories this week?', 'What have we got new today?' and 'I want a much better news list tomorrow.' These questions are often aggressively put and have to be instantly answered. And if the answer is not satisfactory, a tirade can ensue. Andy was the most demanding of all the editors I worked for – but possibly the best journalist of his generation, and the most inspiring.

In business these days, such behaviour has been turfed out. But in newspapers, this raw, high-octane style of management is par for the course. I never felt bullied or intimidated by it. I thought it was the norm.

My style was quieter by comparison. I don't think a single reporter ever saw me lose my temper with them or even shout at them, and my relatively softer management style was probably one of the many reasons why I never progressed beyond news editor.

Rebekah had a different management style to Andy when she was editor. An underperforming subordinate would be met with a series of pointed questions, punctuated by a lengthy, unnerving, ice-cold stare. It normally did the trick! She was extremely demanding and knew precisely what she wanted in the paper. And she was possessed of a campaigning zeal seldom seen among editors.

Between Rebekah and Andy, from 1996 to 2007, when they variously occupied the posts of editor and deputy editor, the *News of the World* was an incredibly fast-paced and interesting place to work and they commanded huge loyalty among staff.

But, as much as I enjoyed working for them, the news desk was not for me. Fifty stories, fifty problems – and none of them of your own making. I made no secret of it. I also disliked being rooted to a desk after so long as a roving reporter, and sitting in an office with no windows. I hated it. Andy called me into his office in April 2003 and said he would take me off the desk, and he asked me what I wanted to do. He suggested New York. That was out of the question for me with my young family. So chief reporter was offered. I seized it with gusto, and so began the most exciting and fulfilling part of my career.

CHAPTER 17

THE DAVID BECKHAM AFFAIR: TO AUSTRALIA

MY OFFICE TELEPHONE rang and Andy Coulson's secretary Belinda Sharrier asked me to come straight to his office, as a big story had come into the *News of the World*. I took my notepad and walked across the newsroom floor to the editor's office.

Coulson sat behind his imposing desk. His deputy, Neil Wallis, sat next to him on a leather sofa. Both wore serious faces. Andy spoke first, not to outline the details of the story but to impress upon me the secrecy of the operation he wanted me to carry out. No one in the office was to be told about the job apart from the managing editor, Stuart Kuttner. Even the news editor, Gary Thompson, and his deputy, Ricky Sutton, were to be kept out of the loop for the time being.

I was to fly to Australia to meet a young woman by the

name of Sarah Marbeck who was claiming to friends that she had been involved in an affair with the Manchester United and England football captain David Beckham.

The tip had come in from a top Melbourne lawyer called Mike Brereton, whose clients included Kylie Minogue, so it was coming from a reputable source. Mike was representing her and my first port of call was to meet him at his offices.

The cloak of secrecy around the operation meant I couldn't even use our travel agency to book and pay for my flights and accommodation. Absolutely no one on Fleet Street had to know where I was or why. Everything had to be paid for by me and claimed back from the company at the end of the job. Even my closest family were asked not to reveal to anyone that I was in Melbourne. In those days, even if a rival newspaper simply discovered my whereabouts, they would despatch a reporter to try to find out what I was doing, suspecting a big story they could piggy-back on.

Coulson, who was a stickler for confidentiality and secrecy, asked me to send all updates only to himself and Wallis via email. It's not unusual for Fleet Street newspapers to throw a cloak of secrecy around its big exclusives. Newspapers are notoriously leaky. Many sub-editors and photographers are freelancers who work on several newspapers. Occasionally, a fragment of information overheard at one newspaper can suddenly find itself emerging in the newsroom of another. Then, with a bit of jig-sawing and probing, your closely guarded and hard-won scoop ends up gracing the front page of a rival newspaper.

On a Sunday newspaper such as the *News of the World*, your scoops are especially vulnerable. You might have the story ready to run on a Tuesday but have to wait five more days to publish it, leaving the dailies four publishing days to discover what you're up to and steal the story from right under your nose. Nothing is more frustrating to a Sunday newspaper journalist than to see a story that has cost thousands of pounds and many weeks to investigate appearing in the *Daily Mail* or the *Daily Mirror* on a Saturday morning. It happened many times and led to countless bad-tempered post mortems and irrational blame games.

I went to see Kuttner about a cash advance and he gave me £3,000, although the next few weeks were going to cost many thousands more. It was agreed that my platinum American Express card would be able to fund the rest for the time being. Melbourne was a 23-hour flight and I had to hit the ground running, so I asked Kuttner's permission to fly business class and he agreed.

Sitting in the editor's office was a little like being in a goldfish bowl. The floor-to-ceiling glass window overlooking the newsroom meant the news desk executives and reporting team could see who was speaking to the editor and whether it was friendly or fierce.

The high-level summit between myself, the editor and his deputy – and the seriousness with which it was being conducted – had alerted several of the more observant members of staff to the fact that something big was afoot. As I made my way across the floor and out of the building, several curious reporters were eager to find out and approached me with a casual 'Everything alright Nev?' This was designed to elicit a 'Yes, fine, I'm off to do a story on Joe Bloggs,' or a 'No, terrible. I've just been fired for stealing the petty cash.' Instead, I threw them off the scent with a grumble, moaning: 'I'm the lousy tail-end Charlie on someone else's crummy story,' which was boring enough for them to sit back down and forget all about it after shuddering at the memory of being in a similar position themselves.

I drove back to my home in Esher, Surrey, packed a bag and set off for the airport and after a long flight, I landed in Melbourne. I headed straight for Brereton's office in the smart part of the city, where I was to meet both him and Sarah for the first time.

Brereton was the typical showbiz lawyer. In his early fifties, but trendy, charming and highly sociable. He loved nothing better than combining business with pleasure, and over the next few weeks I would spend many hours with him in the city's nightclubs, bars and restaurants. His high-rolling, hard-living lifestyle had led to a pale, jaded countenance, but he always seemed to have a very glamorous girl, often thirty years younger, on his arm.

Brereton's secretary, Kristen, introduced me to Sarah for the first time in a small office high up and overlooking the old tramlines, trams and the overhead cables that powered them.

The first thing that struck me about Sarah was her

resemblance to the late Hollywood actress Ava Gardner, with her dark, sultry good looks, high-arched eyebrows and appealing, oval-shaped eyes. She was twenty-nine but, unlike many young women of her generation, she dressed stylishly too. A Malaysian-born daughter of a barrister, she had an exotic, athletic poise and impeccable manners.

Brereton had been promised £100,000 for the publication of her story, so he was keen that we both got on with the job of proving she was telling the truth and getting it into the paper. That would involve a series of lengthy interviews to obtain the details of her story and also to see if there were any inconsistencies in her tale that would set alarm bells ringing. She wouldn't have been the first girl to try to cash in on a bogus tale of an affair with a married celebrity. When her story was recorded on tape, I would then set about trying to get her to speak to Beckham on the phone and hopefully record crucial admissions which would confirm her story to be true – or, failing that, communicate with him by text.

It was a simple and brutally effective plan. I'm afraid in the world of tabloid journalism such methods are vital as without significant proof of this nature, newspapers are open to highly damaging libel suits. A successful libel suit from Beckham would have cost the paper millions and its editor and chief reporter their jobs.

Coulson had calculated that if we got the story wrong, it would have led to a record-breaking libel action with Beckham, one of the highest-paid soccer stars in the world. The damage to his image, which had been carefully crafted as a solid family man and loyal husband, could lead to him losing lucrative sponsorship deals worth millions of pounds. And it would be the *News of the World* that would have to compensate him. But it was Beckham's cultivated image that was to prove the reason for his downfall. Few people have questioned the morality of exposing Beckham's secret affairs, and in the days, weeks and months that followed my exposés, every newspaper in Britain, every tabloid and broadsheet, and many abroad, followed every twist and turn in the saga. This was because there was a perception that the public had been deceived into buying into the Beckham fairy tale and parting with their cash to watch him or buy the products he endorsed. The Beckhams had married in rather vulgar fashion, some might say, on his and hers 'thrones'. But, like all fairy tales, it was fanciful and false. And we believed it was in the public interest for us to say so.

Both Coulson and Wallis were emphatic I had to get it right. Not one inaccuracy. I had never been sued for libel in my career. Nor had I been censured by the Press Complaints Commission for any inaccuracies in any of my stories, despite the highly public and scandalous nature of many of them. That still remains the case today (touch wood!).

Coulson very kindly said to me before I left for Australia: 'You're the safest pair of hands I've got', and added that if the story was there to be had, he was certain that I was one of the few people capable of getting it. Wallis warned me that I would probably be holed up with Sarah for several weeks and he believed I was the best equipped to deal with tantrums and potential walk-outs. If Coulson was all strategy, Wallis was all psychology, and together they made a formidable team. I've never been regarded as a very sociable person but I've always managed to bumble along in a fairly affable fashion with colleagues and interviewees. In fact, I can only ever recall having one fallout in my career, despite my often rather outspoken and provocative style. Keeping all parties on board during what would turn out to be an emotional roller-coaster for them was going to be crucial and Wallis spotted that.

I estimated it could take up to two weeks and booked two suites at the Crowne Plaza Hotel for the duration. The hotel was one of the most expensive in the city but we calculated we had to keep Sarah happy and occupied during what could be a very laborious exercise. So, in between lengthy and detailed interviews and re-interviews, she had a gym, swimming pool, beauty treatments and so forth. And in the evening, the hotel had several restaurants providing a whole range of different international cuisines. Sarah and I decided we would have fun, swimming and running in the mornings and enjoying laughter and drinks in equal measures in the evenings as we worked on the story.

If the clandestine nature of the operation was usual to me, the out-of-pocket expenses were not. In all, from September 2003 to April 2004, I spent £45,285.38 out of my own pocket and returned the £3,000 advance intact to Kuttner, an act of honesty unheard of in Fleet Street! So irregular was my financial conduct, there was no known system for the return of a cash advance at News International. It was the usual practice for reporters to miraculously account for every penny and return empty handed. Kuttner and his secretary spent an hour talking to accounts about how it could be returned and a system was set up. From that day forth, Kuttner, famously a brutal slasher of expenses, rarely chopped a penny from mine.

The morning after our first meeting, Sarah turned up at the hotel with enough clothes and cigarettes for two weeks. I ordered tea and we started our taped interview. It was an interview that would form the basis of one of the most read stories in the history of newspapers.

Sarah sat in one of the armchairs, inhaled deeply on one of her ever present Marlboro Lights and began her tale, unblushingly and in eye-watering detail.

She said:

> Sleeping with David Beckham was a momentous day for me, not just a one-night stand.
>
> I certainly didn't take our affair lightly and nor did he. This is probably the most famous father, family man and husband in the world and he changed my life.
>
> I know I meant something to him because, on and off, we continued our relationship month after month after month. When we made love, David told me, 'I know what we're doing is wrong, but I can't help it.'

The first time he took me to bed he kissed me everywhere. I looked down and there was David Beckham kissing my breasts! David Beckham!

She revealed that they first met at a party thrown by Singapore socialites Frank and Mavis Benjamin during Manchester United's pre-season tour of the Far East in 2001. It was 26 July.

And they had their picture taken just four hours before falling into bed together.

Sarah, who had worked as a model for Armani, Gucci and Calvin Klein, explained:

I was invited to the party through my modelling agency. The Benjamins have a palatial house, and I first saw David as I was walking down the stairs to the pool. He just stood there staring at me. So I went up to him and said, 'Hi, how do you find Singapore weather?'

He complained, 'It's a bit hot.'

I started laughing at his outfit – all the players had been told to wear white T-shirts and shorts. He agreed: 'We all look stupid.' Soon, David asked me to meet him in the private movie theatre under the house. He'd obviously checked the place out.

We sat at the back and I asked, 'How's your wife?'

He said, 'She's fine, yeah, she's well.' Then he said to me, 'Look, I don't usually do this but I'd really like your company later tonight. Will you come to my room on your own?'

He gave her his room number at the Shangri-La Hotel but the conversation was cut short when a bodyguard came into the room and told Beckham that the United bus was ready to leave. 'I didn't know what to do,' said Sarah.

> I stayed at the party another half an hour thinking about it, then I thought, 'Right, I'm going to go through with it.'
> I ran back to my apartment and got changed into a T-shirt and wide-leg purple cargo pants. I didn't wear any make-up because I didn't want him to think I was getting dressed up for him. But I did put on nice lingerie 'just in case' – black lacy Calvin Klein bra and knickers.

At the hotel, Sarah discovered she was expected. She was escorted to a room and suddenly received a startling insight into the secret world of soccer stardom. She explained:

> There were some players I didn't recognise. They told me to sit with them for a while and someone would be seeing me soon. I asked them why the secrecy and they just said this was the way it always was.
> Then this big bodyguard came in and said, 'OK, are you ready? I'm going to take you up now. But I'm going to have to take your bag and shoes.' He was treating me like a terrorist. We went up a couple of floors and knocked on a door.
> David opened it and gave me a big smile. He closed the

door behind me and said of the security, 'Look, I'm really sorry. That's just the way it is. Would you like a cup of tea?'

Beckham told Sarah that United boss Alex Ferguson always made sure alcohol was taken out of minibars.

'It was a bit awkward at first,' she said. 'I sat in a chair and he sat on the bed, the TV was on. Then I said, "Well, now what?" Without saying anything, he gently took my hand and led me to the bed. He lay down and asked me to lie down too.'

As she settled onto the duvet, Sarah noticed a card on the table from the hotel. It read: 'Welcome David Beckham. Please give our best wishes to your wife and child.'

She had little time to feel uncomfortable. 'After a few seconds he started kissing me,' she said.

I liked it. Then he started kissing my legs before he turned me round again and started kissing my hair and neck. He said he loved my neck and kept saying how beautiful and long it was. I was becoming very aroused.

Then he gave me a very slow full body massage. It was so sexy. He kept saying he loved my long legs.

He slid his hand inside my trousers and said he thought the fabric of my knickers felt nice. 'Can I see them?' he asked. By now I certainly wanted him to see them. I sat astride him and began to explore his body too. I could feel he was very aroused.

We fantasised on the bed about having sex. I told him

I'd like to be taken by surprise and to be made love to fast and furious while he held my face in his hands. It made him more and more excited.

He said he wanted to make love to me and said if I did, I'd never want another man. But it wasn't cheesy, it was wonderful.

Our hands were everywhere, inside each other's clothes. Then he took my top off and when we were both naked we made love. It was perfect, really passionate.

I've no idea how long it lasted – when you're in bed with David Beckham, you're not looking at the clock, believe me. He liked to be on top and that was absolutely fine by me.

He said he felt he'd been hit by a sledgehammer from the first time he saw me. He said he loved the way I tied my hair back.

At 3 a.m. she was ready to go home and asked for the bodyguard to return her belongings.

'David wanted me to stay the night but I needed to be on my own to get my head together,' she added.

Beckham was so confident his fans and the media wouldn't suspect him of cheating, he invited Sarah to join him in the players' tunnel after an international match.

The date was 27 March 2002 and Beckham was leading England against Italy at Leeds United's Elland Road ground.

There he was in his England strip, all hot and sweaty, just minutes after the game. He had a big smile on his face.

We made fantastic love and he gave me the highest, most intense moments of passion I've ever felt.

At the crucial moment his eyes were blazing and he threw his head back in ecstasy. It was an amazing experience for both of us. He certainly understands a woman's body. He knows when to pick up the pace or slow down, and exactly where to position himself. He wanted to make sure I was satisfied – and, believe me, I was.

Sarah, besotted with Beckham after he seduced her in Singapore, had contacted her lover and told him she was flying to Britain and would be staying with an aunt in Leeds.

'David said he was very excited,' she said.

He told me, 'I'm looking forward to seeing you.' He also told me what he wanted to do to me in bed – and when he said that, I couldn't wait to see him.

He left me tickets for the game at the ground's ticket desk. I went with my cousin and we had great seats close to the pitch.

England lost 2–1, but Beckham was desperate to see his girlfriend.

Sarah said:

After the match, a guard came to my seat and asked if I was Sarah and told me to follow him. That's when he took me to the players' tunnel.

All the other players were there so he couldn't kiss me, but I was so happy to be there I didn't care.

David went off to shower and texted her a little while later asking her to come to the Oulton Hall Hotel, a grand Victorian mansion near Leeds where the team was staying.

'I put on a nice pair of boots and sexy black underwear,' said Sarah.

My cousin Matthew drove me there and it suddenly dawned on him what was happening when we saw the England team buses parked up outside.

I went in alone and waited in the foyer. It was about 9.30 p.m. I texted him to say I'd arrived and he texted me back telling me to come up to his room.

David opened the door in his white T-shirt and a pair of sports shorts. His hair was a bit longer than the last time I'd seen him but he still looked gorgeous.

This time there were no security guards around but he didn't want me to hover in the hallway. 'Come in quick,' he said.

Then he just looked at me and said, 'I can't believe you're here, Sarah. I can't believe I'm staring at you again and we're alone.'

It was a magic moment. He held me tight and kissed me

so tenderly straight away. I'd been dying for that.

We had no inhibitions: the lights stayed on. We made love right there on the bed. He took his clothes off first, and stood in front of me naked. I was wearing jeans and a turtleneck sweater and I slipped out of them and joined him on the bed.

He has a very nice, toned, athletic body and he's well endowed. You might say he's a very genetically blessed man. Even his feet are gorgeous. I know if most women saw David Beckham naked they wouldn't be looking at his feet but I wanted to check out every single inch of him.

We started kissing each other all over, and then he began giving me oral sex. He had a very sensual technique.

Finally we made love on the bed, going through a whole variety of positions, though he was on top most of the time. He kept nibbling my ear, which made me giggle. There was a lot of kissing – a lot of tongues.

He didn't talk about what he was going to do, he just did it. All he said was: 'You're really beautiful.'

Afterwards we lay there cuddling. We didn't really chat, just lots of cuddles. It was a lovely room and a really comfortable bed.

By now it was 2 a.m. 'My cousin was still waiting downstairs so I said I had to go,' she said.

This time David didn't ask me to stay the night. He said, 'If we get caught, I'll be in a lot of trouble.' As I left he promised to see me again and told me, 'I'll find some time for us to hang out properly while you're still in the country.'

Three days later, Becks arranged for Sarah and her cousin to watch Leeds at home to Man United. The tickets were in the name of then Leeds star Jonathan Woodgate.

But despite this, she did not see Beckham alone again. 'I went south to London but we never got together,' she said. 'He told me he was busy.'

But even after their Oulton Hall meeting, the text messages and phone calls continued, only tapering off from around the time Victoria gave birth to son Romeo on 1 September 2002. 'Throughout our time we rarely talked about football,' said Sarah.

> He never mentioned Sir Alex Ferguson or the England manager Sven to me. I think he knew I wasn't that interested.
>
> But he did send me a text straight after England beat Germany 5–1 in September 2001. He said, 'Nothing makes me happier than playing football!'
>
> It was such an historic moment for English fans that I was really proud to hear from him. I asked him how he felt playing in front of millions of people, if he was nervous and he said, 'It's a piece of p*ss.'
>
> Most of the time we'd just tease each other. I teased him

about all the advertising he was doing and said, 'Everywhere I go I see your face.' He thought that was funny, but he knew I loved his Police sunglasses ads.

I remember towards the end of our time together he rang me after a long period of no contact and I said to him, 'Have you been texting all your other girls and finally got back round to me?'

He said, 'Don't be silly.'

Beckham was clearly besotted with his young girlfriend and the pair enjoyed texting and had fairy-tale pet names for each other as they texted erotic messages.

He was 'Peter Pan'. Sarah was 'Tinkerbell' … and David's wife Victoria was 'Wendy'.

Beckham sent her hundreds of messages over two years, many of them intensely sexual and explicit.

The lovers start using fairy-tale names in texts on 2 August 2001, days after they first had sex. Becks's text was sent at 3.50 a.m.

> **DB:** Is my fairy awake yet?
> **SM:** This is fairy-tale stuff, baby. If I am your fairy like Tinkerbell – what must you be, my Peter Pan? So tell me sugar, how's Wendy?
> **DB:** You are right it is fairy-tale stuff, and as for Wendy all I can think about is Tinkerbell, and as for the making love 24:7 and the goodbyes, we can make that work. It has too!!
> **DB:** Wendy helps me write the messages. Just joking, she's far away.

And in response to a question from Sarah:

> **DB**: Wendy who? All I can think about is Tinkerbell. I can't be a*sed talking to Wendy. Explain that one.

His Peter Pan messages now came thick and fast…

> **DB**: Tinkerbell is the one doing it for Peter Pan. When Peter Pan and Tinkerbell are together that is when things start getting so cheeky.

> **DB**: Tinkers when you are here anything goes!

By the end of the month he was expressing his love.

> **DB**: I know Peter adores Tinkers but I also know Tinkers loves Peter! :) X

But in January 2002, disaster struck.

> **DB**: Wendy found them. The messages that u sent to me she saw about 6.

But he still kept texting:

> **DB**: I miss u Tinkers.

Mobile phone memory cards detailing Becks's texts showed that he began messaging her in earnest on 31 July 2001, five days after they met.

DB: I need to c u so bad, I need that neck … I'm still feeling that electricity! Are you? I wanted u the first time I saw u. XX

The following day there was a succession of texts:

DB: I want my mouth in more places the next time. I don't know what we are doing but the funny thing is I don't want it to stop. X

DB: First of all your neck, then it would be your *******, then I would make love to you for some time and at the end I would turn you around and **** you from ****** whilst pulling at that gorgeous hair then a cuddle and a kiss. X

DB: You like being taken by surprise u like your calfs massaged u like the *****, you like it nice and slow but u also like it fast and furious!

On 4 August 2001, Becks was texting enthusiastically.

DB: When we see each other next it will be my eyes, my hands and my teeth undressing that gorgeous body

DB: I can't wait to kiss u head to toe then sit you down and **** your ******* and **** you till you are so *** u can't take any more and I would bend u over and **** u so hard :) X

DB: The hardest thing is missing you and wanting you but not being able to have you!

Two days later, Sarah has heard a rumour that Beckham had three-in-a-bed sex after she left him at the Singapore hotel and quizzes him:

DB: It was hard enough getting you in my room let alone 2 girls. Anyway I promised I'd never done this before and I meant it.

Forty-eight hours later he adds:

DB: The two girl thing is still p***ing me off, trust me I've never been tempted. I've only met ONE person that really does it for me.

On 12 August, he was being very secretive.

DB: I can't talk cause I don't want someone to hear, but what I could do is answer and just listen to you and reply with a um. I know it's pathetic and it will sound like your on the phone to a pervert heavy breathing, but remember I haven't told anyone and don't intend anyone finding out, **** this is stupid. X

A few days later he and Sarah exchange texts while he was being driven in a car.

DB: My friends in my car are wondering why I have just burst out laughing and have gone red, **** that was sexy, and **** I miss u too! X

The following day, 16 August, there were more:

DB: I'm sat in a park with some friends chilling, and all I can think about is you and I'm also being asked who I'm texting. For your information you're my mum!

242

Late in August they start teasing:

> **DB:** Tell me what's your favourite part of yourself! X
> **SM:** My legs on your's
> **DB:** My favourite part of me has to be my ****!

The texts continued for the rest of the year. By January 2002 he was trying to persuade her that he is 'faithful' in only having her as a mistress.

> **DB:** What surprises me is I'm so, so faithful, I mean I don't even look at a woman, I admire mens looks more than women not in that way but u get where I'm coming from.

On 10 January came three vital words:

> **DB:** I love you. X

But by February, he was back to sex.

> **DB:** We won't last long clothed. I'm going to spend ages tasting u and cant wait for u to taste me…

Later that day he adds:

> **DB:** I'd love to be with u now just to let my fingers slide over your ******* while my ****** is sliding over your ******* making

u even more ****er than u are now, then I would slide my body up your ***** legs and then ***** myself **** ****** *** and make love. X

But by late August 2002, the affair was fading and he was beginning to let her down gently and explaining the increasing gaps between messages:

DB: I told u it was going to be hard and im sorry but sometimes its not possible.

I pored over the texts for clues that Sarah's story could be bogus, but everything added up. She had the ticket for the Leeds *v.* Manchester United game, in the name of Jonathan Woodgate, the Leeds centre back. And the team did indeed stay at the Oulton Hall Hotel that night. Then there was the photo of them together at the Singapore party. And hundreds of texts over a two-year period from a man who claimed to be a footballer who is having sex with her. But it wasn't anywhere near enough evidentially. We had no way of discovering who the phone was registered to or that it was ever in Beckham's possession.

So without that proof, we needed to fall back on my original plan to tape a telephone call to him and record vital admissions of fact. Beckham had been noticeably cooler and less frequent in his texts by September 2003. In fact, there had been none for several weeks. Sarah had never previously telephoned him so a call out of the blue would have looked very suspicious. On my instruction, she began texting him. There was no reply to her first text, so we decided to play it cool and leave it for a couple of days before trying again. No reply. Another few days later we tried a third time, again with no reply. This went on for five long weeks with absolutely no response.

The decision to stay so long was because the tabloid end of Fleet Street had long regarded this particular story as being the biggest scoop imaginable. I filled in my time reading, running, swimming and playing tennis. I also palled up with Brereton and his friends, drinking and going to Aussie Rules games. I came to really enjoy the company of Australians. Their irreverent banter and classlessness appealed to me. I liked the way Brereton, a brilliant, highly educated lawyer, surrounded himself with barristers, retired policemen, publicans and a host of ordinary Joes and yet you couldn't tell who wore the overalls and who the judge's wig. But all the time, Sarah was either by my side or in the adjoining suite in case that all-important text came through and we managed to get our quarry on the phone line.

It never did. And with no proof, we had no story, and it was frustrating. It was also puzzling, as Beckham had been a prolific texter for two years and there had been no fallout between them.

By late October 2003, I was on the plane home and very glad indeed of that business class ticket and flat bed. I was also glad of the complimentary bottle of champagne the steward gave me while we were stranded on the runway for an hour during a fierce electrical storm. And of the second one as soon as we were airborne! Two bottles of champagne went down in two hours; I forgot the frustration and failure of the past five weeks and slept soundly.

Beckham's last contact had been out of the blue, when he phoned her on 23 August 2003.

Sarah said:

> I told him that it had been many months without contact and he insisted he'd sent me loads of messages but that I couldn't have received them.
>
> But he clearly kept my phone number all this time. We talked a bit about his move to Real Madrid and then he said he had to go.
>
> I don't know if I'll ever hear from him again.

She didn't. Beckham had now moved on to another extremely glamorous young woman, who was working as his personal assistant: Rebecca Loos.

CHAPTER 18

THE DAVID BECKHAM AFFAIR: TO SPAIN AND REBECCA LOOS

BY MARCH 2004, the Beckham story seemed dead in the water and we had put it behind us. In Fleet Street, for every great scoop there are many failures that fall by the wayside and we never dwell on the big ones that elude us.

I was wrapping up a story in Dorset when Coulson called me on my mobile. Could I drop everything and head into the office, where he would brief me on a story? In the meantime, I was not to speak to anyone in the office, even the news editor, about the planned briefing or what would come out of it. I motored back as fast as I could, walked into Coulson's office and found him looking deadly serious behind his desk once again.

He explained that Beckham had just ended an affair with his PA Rebecca Loos and I was to try to link up with her in Madrid and prove the story. Rebecca had been dumped by the Beckhams after Victoria became suspicious and she had indicated she might be willing to talk about it. Most importantly, there were hundreds of texts from him on her phone. If they came from the same number as he used to text Sarah Marbeck, there was also the possibility that we would prove Sarah's story too. As with the Marbeck investigation, there was to be total silence about the case and it all had to be funded by me.

It also became clear why Beckham had been ignoring Sarah Marbeck's texts. On 18 September 2003, when I was holed up with Sarah in Australia, Beckham was photographed with a mystery girl inside and outside a Madrid nightspot.

On 28 September, the *News of the World* ran the photographs. But what we didn't know was that the mystery girl was Rebecca Loos. And after they left the nightclub, they went back to his hotel to make love for the first time, embarking on a torrid affair. Sarah Marbeck was the last thing on his mind. This explained Beckham's puzzling silence and the failure of my Australian venture.

The pictures had caused fury in the Beckham household. Rebecca was dumped and, after much thinking, she had approached the publicity agent Max Clifford, wanting to explore the matter further. Clifford came to us and we signed Rebecca up for £100,000.

Coulson's cheerless expression disguised the fact that he

must have been doing mental somersaults for joy at the prospect of landing one of the biggest tabloid stories for years.

Every News International editor is desperate to prove to Rupert Murdoch that he is at the top of his game. And when it came to the *News of the World*, Rupert liked nothing better than it setting the agenda and being the talking point of the nation as the scoop rolled out. This Beckham story would do both and define Coulson's editorship.

But if Coulson was jumping for joy, he didn't show it. I have known him for twenty-eight years and he was as tightly wrapped as a nineteen-year-old as he is now. Cool, analytical, polite, betraying little emotion and utterly focused. When people read the cheeky-chappie headlines of *The Sun* or the *News of the World*, they often think they are fun places to work where everyone is chuckling over their computers and nothing is taken too seriously. Nothing could be further from the truth. Coulson reflected the ethos of the *News of the World*: 'Get it – but get it right.' But as I left his office for Madrid, he did betray one sign of inner excitement, one glimpse that he believed we were onto a story that would propel us all onto the world stage. On every story, it was a given that a *News of the World* reporter would go the extra mile and do everything in his or her power to bring the story home. By the time you ended up at the *News of the World*, that was taken for granted. But as we parted, he looked at me and said, 'I really, really want this story to work, Nev. I know you'll do everything you can. Take your time, just make sure we get it absolutely right.'

En route to the airport, I called Rebecca and arranged to meet her that night in the basement of an unfashionable bar in Madrid. It was almost midnight when I arrived and we sat at a corner table to discuss business.

My first impression of Rebecca was that although she had spent most of her life in Spain, she would have fitted perfectly into the Chelsea social scene. Her mother was English and her father was a Dutch diplomat but she had received a private education at Madrid's exclusive Runnymede College. She was also a very nice-looking girl, with the understated elegance that is frequently seen among female professionals in Spain (they quietly mock their British counterparts for their poor dress sense, especially their 'clumpy shoes'!).

She was also very bright, obtaining eleven GCSEs and three A levels, and learning several languages before moving into a glittering career in banking and, later, PR.

By twenty-five, she was headhunted by Beckham's management company SFX to look after the Beckhams.

She was just as interested to meet me as I was her, I was to discover. She was extremely wary about speaking to the *News of the World* and wanted to find out if she could trust me. She was preparing to sell her most intimate secrets to a tabloid newspaper and it didn't come naturally to her. That one-hour meeting over a glass of wine was crucial as she later told me that if she had been confronted with a brash, pushy type, she would have walked away. Luckily, we gelled. In fact, we have remained friends ever since.

I was very frank with her. I explained there would need to be significant evidence to run the story and she would have to be prepared to make taped telephone calls to Beckham. She understood and we agreed to meet the following day to start work.

I checked into the InterContinental and booked three suites under a false name to prevent any opposition reporters finding me if they got wind of the story. A few hours later, I was joined by Conrad Brown, who would take covert video and still footage if Beckham decided to meet Rebecca. Conrad did a lot of our undercover video work and had learned his trade from his father, the late, great *News of the World* reporter Gerry Brown. I had worked with both father and son on assignments for years and found them deeply impressive. I was beginning to feel quite confident about our prospects. I had the main player onside, I had an excellent undercover cameraman, and I had the time and resources to complete the task. Beckham had also been texting Rebecca in the run-up to our meeting so it looked likely we could at least observe a text conversation and ultimately record a phone conversation. And hopefully they would contain crucial admissions that would provide the evidence needed to run the story.

Our first plan was simply to wait for Beckham to text Rebecca and take it from there. Rebecca had never been the first to text and to have done so now may have raised his suspicion. While we were waiting, Rebecca and I went through every detail of her story on tape and I sent over the transcripts to Coulson and Wallis, who were delighted.

But there was one piece of evidence that looked extremely promising. Rebecca showed me all the explicit text messages Beckham had sent her. They came from a series of different numbers. I cross-checked them with the numbers that had been used to send texts to Sarah Marbeck and found that one of them matched.

All we needed to do was prove this number belonged to David Beckham to prove his fairy-tale marriage was a sham, as he had been having affairs with two women, almost simultaneously. But this was to prove extremely difficult. Beckham changed his phone number like other men changed their socks, and this one was long discarded and was now a dead number.

The days ticked by and nothing came from Beckham. Then a week. Then two weeks. It was beginning to get a little dull, too. I couldn't move around freely in Madrid. British sports reporters were frequent visitors due to Beckham's presence and if they spotted me, they would know immediately I was onto the only story that would interest the *News of the World* in Madrid – a David Beckham scandal. This would send Fleet Street rushing to Madrid to try to piggy-back onto my story. And sports reporters, eager to curry favour with Beckham, would delight in blowing my cover.

If the investigation was to survive, there was nothing to do other than lie doggo at the hotel, even taking all our meals in our rooms. Eventually, owing to the amount of money I was spending at the hotel due to our extended stay, I managed to upgrade us to VIP status. This allowed us access to a VIP lounge, not unlike those for first-class airline travellers. Here, we could relax over a drink in the safe knowledge that the zone would be out of the budget of travelling reporters and cameramen.

People often assume the job of a roving reporter working undercover for a big Sunday newspaper is a glamorous one. But it is a life spent trawling over tiny bits of hard-won evidence and trying to persuade people to part with information they would rather keep hidden from you. It is also a solitary existence, spent apart from the rest of Fleet Street, which hunts as a garrulous and devil-may-care pack. Many find it lonely. And working on your own in the field for weeks at a time means you have to be totally self-motivating. Although the job suited me, it didn't feel glamorous in the slightest. At the back of my mind was a rather puritanical, northern sense of whether I was giving value for money. I always saw myself as part of the bottom line, and if I failed on a story I had an acute sense of being a very expensive overhead that had produced nothing for the paper that week. Coupled with that was the ever present understanding that one long fallow period or one big mistake and you were out the door. Very often, one would lead to the other. The pressure to produce ended up breaking marriages, and drove many to drink or drugs or out of the industry altogether. By 2004, aged just forty-two, I was already the longest-serving reporter on the paper. Thankfully, I was still happily married, drug-free and a moderate drinker!

I've often compared my job to that of a professional footballer. Few footballers will tell you they actually enjoy playing the game. The pressure to produce without the hint of a mistake ensures that. And losing compounds the misery. It is only in victory that satisfaction lies.

By March 2004, victory on the Beckham front seemed a long way off. On 11 March, ten bombs ripped through the heart of four trains at Madrid railway station, killing 191 commuters and injuring 2,050. They had been exploded by an al-Qaeda-inspired terrorist cell. It was an appalling tragedy and the single worst terrorist attack in Europe. The rush hour blasts rocked the hotel and the streets were screaming with ambulances, fire engines and police cars. A few hours later, as I strolled through the lobby, I heard a voice behind me, 'Hey, Nev!' Fleet Street had arrived to cover the story and someone who knew me had spotted me. Without breaking step and without looking back, I carried on and into the lift to my room. And here I stayed, living on room service, reading books and chatting to Rebecca until the story was done and the British journalists packed up and went home a few days later.

By now, it looked increasingly unlikely that Beckham was going to voluntarily text Rebecca. Coulson was desperate to push the story forward and for us to precipitate a text from him by initiating one. For several days, I had been advising against this on the grounds that Rebecca had *never* initiated a text or phone conversation and to do so would look suspicious. But there was no holding him back now. We had to do something or we could be waiting around for ever. Rebecca sent an innocuous text, 'Hi, how are you?' and we waited. And waited. And waited. A week went by. Nothing.

By now, Coulson was ready for a final throw of the dice. He called me just before 11 a.m. conference and said: 'Get her to call him, I don't care what he says. Tape the call and if we can prove it's his voice and it's to one of the numbers sending explicit texts, that might be enough for us.'

Rebecca was dead against it. Although she was prepared to sell her story she didn't like the cold-blooded aspect of calling him and taping the call. She was so determined she was on the verge of walking out. Coulson was livid: 'Tell her we have spent thousands on this story so far and it was always going to come down to a phone call so get her on the f****** phone!'

Instead, I decided to play it cool and completely backed off. I suggested we forget about it and go for a drink and some dinner. Over dinner, we laughed and joked as usual and she made fun of my clumsy attempts at filleting a sole meunière. In fact, we talked about everything under the sun apart from Beckham and our investigation.

That night, I called Coulson and explained that I hadn't carried out his request, as I had feared we would have lost Rebecca. He was frustrated but understanding. 'Fine, fine, you are the person on the ground. But she must do it tomorrow or we're pulling the plug on this. Call me the minute the call has gone in.'

The following day when we met up, I tried one more time. Very quietly, I explained that Andy would have me on the next plane home if she wouldn't make the call. The call would be for evidence only and not for publication. To my relief, she agreed.

I started the tape recorder, plugged the earpiece into her ear and she dialled his number using the number withheld facility. The phone rang. He picked it up. But he didn't speak. Silence at his end. Rebecca broke the awkwardness and said, 'Hello. David?' This went on for about thirty seconds. Still he remained silent. Then, suddenly and unexpectedly, he let out a series of little, boyish giggles, then hung up. That was it.

I still can't work out what that was all about. Obviously he was deeply suspicious of any call coming into that particular number for some reason.

I rang Coulson and played the bizarre conversation down the phone for him to hear. 'OK. F****** weirdo! Knock it on the head and come back, Nev.'

That was it. Once again, no taped call. And no way of proving he owned the phone he had used to text Sarah Marbeck and Rebecca: I searched everywhere and there was no record of it existing. I was to return empty handed again after spending £45,000 on the operation, which was probably a *News of the World* record. I was very upset about this. We knew the story was true, two girls receiving extremely similar sex-texts from a man. Both girls claimed they were from Beckham and both girls clearly knew him and could prove it. The story was there but the chief reporter had failed to land it.

I was about to book my flight home when I decided to have one last throw of the dice.

With Rebecca Loos in December 2007, on a flying visit to Madrid.

CHAPTER 19

THE DAVID BECKHAM AFFAIR: THE DRAMATIC EXPOSÉ

DURING MY THREE weeks spent combing through evidence with Rebecca, I had focused heavily on trying to prove that the mobile phone used to text both Sarah and Rebecca had belonged to Beckham.

Rebecca had searched meticulously through all her bagged-up work records and she could find no official record of the phone number being registered to him.

But what if the evidence existed among her personal effects at home? I persuaded Rebecca to invite me back to her house so she could go laboriously through every scrap of paper in her bedroom, the family study and in the attic. It took hours as every drawer, cupboard and coat pocket was rifled through in the seven-bedroom mansion. Virtually the last place to be searched was under her bed. She brought out what looked like a wicker sewing box and lifted the lid. Among a few scraps of paper, payslips and assorted business cards was a small piece of paper bearing two absolutely critical pieces of information. At the top were the company details of Beckham's management company, SFX. And then, written in blue pencil, in Beckham's own hand, was his Christian name and surname followed by a phone number. I pulled out my notebook and checked the number against the one I had for the phone that had texted both girls.

It was the same.

In seven months, I had travelled almost 25,000 miles, spending £45,000 in pursuit of what was regarded as the Holy Grail in tabloid journalism. And right at the death, when I feared I was about to fail with flying colours, thanks to a scrap of paper inside a sewing box under a bed, I was about to break one of the biggest stories in tabloid history.

I phoned Coulson and told him: 'We've cracked it. We're there.' It was the last thing he had expected. He told me to hold the line and hastily arranged a meeting that included Wallis, Kuttner and Tom Crone, the News International head lawyer, and put me on loudspeaker.

After I delivered the breakthrough news, Andy said: 'We'll get a silk to take a look at the evidence but in the meantime, write the story up now and send it over.'

It was Saturday, our deadline day for our Sunday edition

and Coulson planned to splash the story on the front page and fill six more pages inside. I thundered out the copy on my laptop from Rebecca's kitchen table. Midway through, Coulson rang and put me on loudspeaker. The London team had been joined by Michael Silverleaf QC, and we talked through our evidence. Barney Monahan, one of our company lawyers, was also on his way to Spain to top and tail the legal pack with an affidavit from Rebecca, swearing the truth of her story.

Later that evening, the affidavit was sworn, the copy was over and we had to leave the family home as soon as possible. As soon as the story hit the streets in London later that evening, Rebecca's house would be besieged by press and our exclusive 'buy-up' would become the property of everyone else. We had to bail out fast as it was now 7 p.m. and the *News of the World* would reach the streets in the next few hours. Rebecca packed a bag, picked up Bu-Bu, her funny little one-eyed pug, and all three of us jumped into a cab. After checking out of the hotel, I picked up a fast hire car and sped off into the night, leaving the rest of Fleet Street to try to pick up the story from the doorstep of her empty family home a few hours later.

I had no idea where we would go, so I studied the map and decided Sotogrande on the south coast sounded as implausible a place as any to hide out. I put my foot down and headed south at a considerable speed, covering the 400 miles in just short of six hours. A few hours later, in the early hours of the morning, we checked into a remote hotel and waited for the Beckham bombshell to drop on everyone's breakfast tables.

In the morning, I switched on Sky TV to watch the fallout. Nothing. And for the next few hours, every broadcaster steered clear from even mentioning the story. Everyone was extremely wary of any legal repercussions and there was an odd stand-off as everyone waited for one of the major news outlets to take a deep breath and plunge into the story. Coulson called me sounding confused and a little anxious to note the same and said it felt as though we were inhabiting a 'strange twilight zone and a different universe to everyone else'.

The first indication that the story was to go global came as we took our seats outside a local café for an afternoon coffee. There were about a dozen tables, each seating about five or six people crowding around a single copy of the *News of the World*. Each table had an English-speaking Spaniard translating the story for the benefit of the others, who were clearly fascinated by the revelations concerning the Real Madrid superstar. It was a strange sight and my news instinct told me that such frantic interest by the ordinary people in a remote café in some far-flung part of Spain guaranteed that this story would go global. I rang to tell Coulson and he seemed buoyed by the news and also saw it as a weathervane.

The affair was reported in lurid, tabloid detail:

> David Beckham has had a secret torrid affair with an exotic beauty in Madrid, the *News of the World* can reveal.
>
> He took his beautiful personal assistant Rebecca Loos to bed just 90 minutes after this picture of the two of them together was taken at a club.

The lonely England soccer ace turned to the 26-year-old privately educated daughter of a Dutch diplomat for comfort after feeling abandoned by wife Posh in their troubled long-distance marriage.

While Victoria stayed 800 miles away in London concentrating on her recording career, Becks fell head over heels for Rebecca as she worked for him, helping him settle into his transfer to Real Madrid.

Today over the next five pages – in a story that will rock millions of Posh and Becks fans worldwide – we detail how the former Manchester United star secretly made love to Rebecca at two top hotels in the Spanish capital.

How he sent her a stream of graphic text messages telling her what he wanted to do to her in bed.

And how Victoria failed to see the signs that she could be losing her man.

'David is a lonely man in a foreign country,' said a close family friend who Rebecca confided in about her astonishing secret. 'He is a very sensitive guy and is so hurt because Victoria is ignoring him.

'The affair is a surprise to no one who knows him. He's been going weeks without sex, trying to stay faithful to her. But something had to give.'

When we confronted Rebecca – who speaks perfect English – about her relationship, she said: 'I am afraid I have no comment for you. Please leave me alone.'

The *News of the World* first revealed Becks' friendship

with the beauty in a picture exclusive on September 28 last year. That led to fury from Posh and the end of Rebecca's professional involvement with the star couple.

But on the night we spotted them together Becks, 28, kissed Rebecca for the first time after playing a sexy game of Truth or Dare with her and friends at a Thai restaurant before going to Ananda, one of Madrid's top clubs.

Then he swept her off to his suite at the Santa Mauro hotel – to the astonishment of his drivers and bodyguards – for a night of the kind of passion he has been missing with Posh.

'As soon as they got in the room, Rebecca said he seemed a little nervous. He realised he was taking a very big step,' said the friend, spilling the intimate secrets Rebecca had shared with her.

'He held Rebecca's head in his hands and kissed her passionately and said, "I have wanted to be with you like this for so long."

'It was a very powerful moment. He dimmed the lights and started taking his clothes off. Rebecca stripped off too and they stood naked in the middle of the room, kissing passionately.

'David was a sensational lover – their sex was highly charged and explosive. They made love for hours.

'He kept telling her, "I know we shouldn't be doing this but I can't help it. I really want this to happen. It makes me so happy. I want you to stay with me all night long."'

It was the start of a string of trysts between the forlorn soccer star and the well-bred, self-confident stunner.

Becks was truly smitten. 'Rebecca is an attractive and cultured young lady,' says the family friend. 'Although she was born in Madrid, she went to a private English school and walks, talks and dresses like a girl from Chelsea. He really liked that.'

The affair began on September 18 last year after the two had an evening out together. They had been with four of Rebecca's colleagues from SFX Group – the sports personalities management company – at a Thai restaurant.

Becks was at his lowest ebb over his marriage. Victoria was in England with sons Brooklyn and Romeo. Out of his first 89 days in Madrid, Victoria would only spend 35 with him. And he was missing his family.

The friend told us: 'It was a lively evening in the restaurant. David wanted to really let his hair down and he ordered a bottle of champagne. As they all became tiddly, they decided to play Truth or Dare.

'One of David's truth questions turned to sex. The group, including Rebecca, asked him if he had ever had sex on a plane. He said he had but not who with.

'Everyone was amazed how frank he was being. He told everyone, "This is the first time I have had any real fun since I came here two months ago."

'Becks then dared Rebecca to go to the ladies and walk through the entire restaurant with a length of toilet paper dangling from the back of her trousers.

'Rebecca is a fun girl and duly obliged. She even did a

little wiggle in front of the table,' said the family friend. 'David was loving it.

'Later, at the Ananda, David couldn't take his eyes off Rebecca. And he kept gently touching her waist as he guided her through doors.'

It was then that Becks took a telling step away from his marriage. 'He asked her, "Do you want to come back to the hotel suite for a drink with the other four afterwards?"

'Rebecca said she would and he added, with a grin, "Why don't we dump the other four and just come back with me instead?!"

'She was a little stunned but regained her composure quickly with a laugh and a jokey, "**** off!"'

When they left at 3.30 a.m. – an hour after our picture was taken – there were two cars waiting outside.

David, Rebecca and one couple got in one and the other couple followed behind. 'David was determined to get Rebecca back to the hotel discreetly.

'But after they dropped their two passengers off he could wait no longer. He turned to Rebecca and kissed her long and gently.

'Her heart was racing. He was kissing her and caressing her hair and neck. He told her, "I've been waiting ages to do that to you."

'They kissed all the way back to the hotel. David was in a state of high arousal when they got into the bedroom at 4 a.m. and there was no going back. She was lying on her tummy and he kissed her all over.

'She said David's stamina was extraordinary. She could feel his energy pulsating through her as he made love to her on the bed.'

The following night he met her at a tapas bar with her friends. 'David was playing footsie with her under the table,' said the friend.

Once again they went back to the Santa Mauro and his bed. 'Again he said, "I know we shouldn't be doing this but I can't help it. I want this to happen. It makes me so happy."

'The lovemaking was just as passionate as before with David being a little more adventurous.' But a few days later the affair ran into trouble when a rumour went round SFX employees that David and Rebecca had become very close at the Ananda.

When Posh heard, she was livid and telephoned Rebecca to say, 'It is not your job to go out clubbing with my husband so back off.'

Beckham too was given an earbashing from his wife because he phoned Rebecca and said, 'The s**t has hit the fan. Victoria knows what's been going on. We'll have to be careful.'

Their next meeting was on September 22, at Real Madrid star Ronaldo's birthday party at the Brazilian's house. The pair arrived separately to avoid suspicion and hardly spoke to each other all night.

'As they left he texted her, saying, "R u coming back to the hotel?". Rebecca said she would,' added the friend.

'They didn't have full sex that night but decided to experiment, pleasuring each other in a variety of ways involving all manner of kissing and fondling.'

The pair had one more sexual encounter, in December, just before a Real Madrid home game. Beckham asked Rebecca to join him in the Hotel Fenix.

The family friend said: 'It was the least satisfying of all the meetings.' After that tryst Beckham ended his dealings with the SFX Group – and never saw Rebecca again.

The family friend said: 'Rebecca is heartbroken this story has come out but she knew it would eventually. Too many people have seen her texts and they've got into the wrong hands.

'Everyone knows about the affair in the Beckham camp. Rebecca is a very well-bred young woman. She didn't plan this relationship, she's not some starstruck girl.

'But David pursued her and made it very clear that he wanted her sexually. She wasn't in love with him but admitted it was heading that way.'

The 'family friend' was, of course, Rebecca herself, whom we had agreed to disguise as an unwilling participant in the breaking of the story. Following on from this was a whole page of lurid sex texts between Beckham and Rebecca, similar in tone and language to the ones sent to Sarah Marbeck.

By lunchtime, Beckham issued a statement describing the story as 'ludicrous' but stopping short of categorically denying the allegations. This was the green light to the rest of the world that the story was sound and legally safe. The allegations struck at the very heart of the Beckhams' money-spinning family image. If they were false, their lawyers would have stamped on them immediately with a power-fully worded statement along the lines of 'These allegations are completely untrue and are denied by David Beckham, who has instructed us to take legal proceedings against the *News of the World* and any media outlet that repeats them ... blah, blah, blah.'

Max Clifford signposted the weak defence by appearing on TV saying, 'Ludicrous is not the same as saying it's totally untrue. That has made things worse slightly because a lot of media people are thinking, "Well, he didn't come and say it's totally untrue."'

The Beckham statement in full was:

> During the past few months I have become accustomed to reading more and more ludicrous stories about my private life. What appeared this morning is just one further example.
>
> The simple truth is that I am very happily married, have a wonderful wife and two very special kids. There is nothing that any third party can do to change these facts.

The Beckhams never sued us over this story.

As the statement was released, the floodgates began to open.

Sky News were among the first to start headlining on the Beckham story and by the afternoon, virtually every TV station in the world was running it and featuring a copy of our front-page splash, which blazed: 'World Exclusive: Beckham's Secret Affair', with the story running across seven pages.

By mid-afternoon, Coulson, wearing an immaculate cream linen suit, was giving a live interview to Sky, talking through the details of the story and advancing the solid public interest defence we had in running it.

Newspaper reporters and TV camera crews from as far afield as Japan, Russia, Australia and the USA flew into Madrid to try to get a slice of the story for their readers and viewers.

Meanwhile, my phone rang until it was red-hot. Mainly from friends and colleagues on rival newspapers who had been given the thankless and futile task of ringing me in the vague hope that I may give them a steer on where we were. 'Nev, old mate, old pal...' – that sort of thing! I sent everyone away with a friendly but firm flea in their ear – except a couple of reporters who I knew were in the habit of trading information with rivals to try to build up a collective picture together while on big stories. To these two I quietly said, 'in confidence and to go no further', that we were in Madrid, having decided it was easier to hide out in a big city with hundreds of hotels and that Rebecca needed to be close to her family, 'which is a real pain'.

This simple plan worked. Soon dozens of reporters were ringing me trying to squeeze a morsel of new information from me and finishing off with, 'By the way, we know you're in Madrid … you might as well tell us where!'

For the next two weeks, we remained undisturbed 400 miles away while the pack sniffed around a non-existent trail I had laid for them.

I decided we couldn't stay in a hotel as staff would eventually recognise Rebecca, whose face would soon be emblazoned across virtually every newspaper in the world. On the Monday, every British tabloid was splashing on the story. Even the broadsheets filled their pages on the unfolding scandal over the coming weeks. 'Bad news for brand image as Beckham denies affair', said a headline in *The Guardian*. 'Beckham's halo slips', said *The Times*.

I went hunting for a secluded villa where we could base ourselves for the next few weeks and prepare ourselves for the inevitable part two of the Beckham story.

I bypassed estate agents and travel agents to avoid the necessary lodging of passports that could help the smarter reporters find me by ringing around agents. Instead, I found a fairly capacious villa in the middle of nowhere that was for sale. It was empty but I tracked down the owner via a neighbour and asked if he would rent it to me for two weeks. After a certain amount of haggling, he agreed to let me have it for £5,000 cash. It was an impressive, immaculately appointed stone-built affair, with five bedrooms, numerous reception rooms, rolling grounds and a swimming pool. I hired two Spanish ladies to cook and clean for us. We had the perfect self-contained hideaway. Even the grounds couldn't be overlooked, so if a newspaper struck lucky and tracked us down, they wouldn't be able to get that crucial picture of Rebecca. Just one 'live' picture of Rebecca would allow a rival paper to run what we call a 'spoiler' in the industry. That is to say, even without speaking to Rebecca, they could run her picture with a story cobbled together with quotes from friends as she 'prepared to sell her story in this secret Spanish hideaway for a six-figure sum, detailing her torrid love affair with David Beckham ... etc.'

For our Week One splash, headlined 'Beckham's Secret Affair', we had allowed Rebecca the fig leaf of appearing not to have cooperated with our story and seeming to come on board with us with a detailed interview once the story was out, the following week.

So a series of snaps of Rebecca lying by the pool or, worse still, splashing around in it with the chief reporter of the *News of the World*, would have been disastrous for us. Just one picture would have given the dailies the perfect peg to hang the story: 'This is the blonde beauty who tempted David Beckham to stray from wife Posh and spend nights of passion ... etc. etc.'

My reputation and position on the *News of the World* had been cemented for years. And with this story, it was at an all-time high. But make no mistake about it, if I had allowed Rebecca to be pictured by a rival, I would have lost my chief reporter's title at the very least. It is a particular characteristic of Fleet Street for reporters to see their careers crash and burn due to some piece of very public carelessness on the very story that should have sent their star into rapid ascendency. I had to keep my wits about me at all times and Rebecca agreed to abide by a strict curfew.

During the following week, hundreds of thousands of words were written on the Beckham scandal. It was the most talked-about scoop in living memory. Rupert Murdoch was delighted with it. Not only were sales rocketing, but it put his newspaper right at the top of the news agenda throughout the world, something he revelled in. Coulson, Wallis and Kuttner all rang to congratulate me.

Rebekah Brooks (then Wade) also did me the kindness of calling, even though she had left the paper and was now editor of *The Sun*.

But there was still a lot of work to do. We had agreed a £100,000 deal with Rebecca so a part two, this time in her own words – 'the full sit-down', as we say in the industry – had to be obtained. She couldn't hide behind a serious of anonymous quotes for a sum like that. She had to go on the record and this was going to be tricky.

At this point, Coulson showed the sort of managerial qualities that made him one of the most successful editors of his day. Many ego-driven news executives think only of the glory that shines down on them as a result of the hard-won stories of their reporters. Coulson, although an extremely tough character, was very well balanced and a decent human being. Realising it was Easter and that I had been away from home for months on the Beckham saga, he called to tell me to fly my wife and two daughters out to the villa for two weeks – all expenses paid.

As the story flashed around the world, everyone waited for the expected part two. But for two days, I did nothing. No interviews. Just one brief mention that we would have to talk later in the week. Rebecca was quite shaken, albeit slightly euphoric, by the news tsunami she had created. She is also quite a refined soul and I feared the euphoria could easily turn to shock and regret and cause her to pull out.

So for two days, I did my best to shield her from the fallout and keep her grounded. We swam and had a lot of fun in the sun and sampled different Riojas. Tempted by the vast array of high-quality but low-priced Cuban cigars, I foolishly broke a nine-year non-smoking habit – a habit it took me another six years to finally quit.

By Tuesday, it was time to sit down and explain that part two would have to be a full, warts-and-all interview about their affair. Rebecca was realistic and was expecting this. But she wasn't the usual 'kiss and tell' girl who wanted to boast about her famous amour. In fact, she was quite ashamed of it and the last thing she wanted to do was tell the world about it. Every attempt to get her to sit down was met with increasingly greater resistance. Eventually it got to the point where she announced that she wanted to pull out, even if it meant forfeiting the £100,000 fee.

It was a delicate situation. To have Rebecca walk out on me now would have been a disaster. I keep returning to this theme, but such a high-profile story collapse would have been a professional disaster. On Fleet Street, the terms 'safe pair of hands' and 'a good operator' are often bandied about as prerequisites for a staff job. The loss of Rebecca would have fatally damaged my reputation. When I encounter resistance, I usually find the best course of action is to step off the gas and try to tune into their thinking, rather than try to railroad them into following my plan. Most people walk away from high-pressure salesmen in the street. And they do the same to high-pressure reporters, too. Contrary to popular myth, Fleet Street deals are less about aggression and more about the subtleties of human relationships and their psychology. It was very clear to me that the genie was out of the bottle and, sooner or later, Rebecca would realise that she couldn't put it back in. And to walk away now wouldn't make the story go away. But it would lose her the £100,000. Sometimes it's more persuasive for a person to work things out for themselves than to have a reporter try to ram it down their throats.

There was a tense twenty-four hours. Coulson and Wallis thought the £100,000 put them in the driving seat and argued for a much tougher approach. But it is often very near impossible to read the danger signals of a rocky interview from an office 2,000 miles away and seek to rescue it. On this occasion, as with many others, if I encountered editorial resistance to the plan I thought would work, I agreed with the editor's decision – then ignored it completely. The result was, a day later Rebecca was back on side, unpressured and of her own volition. My hands were still deemed 'safe'. And Coulson and Wallis were patting each other on the back for 'saving the day'. Everyone was happy.

That week, slowly, piece by piece, Rebecca revealed the events that had led up to one of the most scandalous affairs in the history of sport or show business. They included some astonishing revelations, including that they had made love in the marital bed and that Beckham had sent the family chauffeur to buy condoms for them. She also revealed that he disliked his wife Victoria's physique, which she claimed had become too skinny for him to find attractive.

The story was accompanied by some superb photographs from Paul Ashton, our chief photographer, one of the best photographers in the business and great company on long-haul jobs like this.

The revelations were eagerly anticipated and they ran across four pages.

But the biggest shock was not provided by Rebecca's sensational revelations.

For, out of the blue and trumping everyone's expectations, there was the splash headline 'I'm Beck's Lover No. 2'.

Spread over seven pages was Sarah Marbeck's graphic account of her affair with Beckham before he met Rebecca. The inside spread on pages 2 and 3 was headlined 'We made love 4 hours after meeting. It sparked two years of txt and passion'. Another two-page spread on pages 4 and 5 was headlined in block capitals 'DAVID BEDDED ME IN ENGLAND TEAM'S

HOTEL'. Pages 6 and 7 were headlined 'I'm Peter Pan, you are Tinkerbell … and poor Posh is Wendy', referring to the code names they had for each other during their 'text-sex sessions'.

Publication of Sarah's story was only made possible by the fact that Beckham had used the phone that we had proved to be his to text Sarah as well as Rebecca. In tabloid terms, it was possibly the most dramatic of editions, certainly within my own memory.

For a second week in a row, the story went global. Sky TV now wanted the first TV interview with Rebecca when we had finished with her, and a hefty financial deal was pulled together. Kay Burley's interview gave Sky One their biggest-ever audience. They very generously offered me £1,000 for pulling it all together. I never accepted payments for tip-offs from rival newspapers and declined. So they very kindly offered me free VIP Sky TV for life, which I gladly accepted. (A deal they were very shabbily to renege on six years later when a new boss came along and could find no record of it.)

News International's chief executive officer Les Hinton was generous in his praise, emailing:

> Neville: What a triumph!
>
> I know you have worked for months on the Beckham story; Andy has kept me up to date as it developed.
>
> I cannot remember the last time a single story so totally consumed all Fleet Street, the rest of the British media and a good chunk of the global media as well.

Seeing us lead the way like this is what we all live for as newspapermen. Thanks very much for such a great job.

Best,
Les

It went on to win me my second Scoop of the Year Award at the British Press Awards.

Andy Coulson was quick to congratulate me, sending a bonus cheque for £1,000 and a short letter to my home, saying:

Dear Neville,

Please find enclosed a bonus cheque … to be used only in relation to some serious self-congratulation.

Your Scoop of the Year award was so deserved. That it has got so far up the nose of all our rivals should prove to you even further what a great hit it was.

Here's to you, Nev. Congratulations once again.

Andy

A few weeks later, he gave me a £10,000 p.a. pay rise out of the blue.

If Coulson was tough and uncompromising, he could also be generous and dish out praise where it was deserved.

He still remains one of the finest newspapermen and most inspiring leaders I have ever worked for.

With the Scoop of the Year Award trophy at the British Press Awards,
March 2005.

CHAPTER 20

A MURDER FOILED

OCCASIONALLY, IN THE murky shallows of tabloid journalism, immense good can be achieved – like saving a human life. I was fortunate to be able to deliver this service to one young lady, whose husband was hell-bent on having her and her lover murdered. It was undoubtedly one of the most important undercover roles I ever performed.

Jasbinder Heer wanted to hire a hitman to bump off his wife Monica, who had left him and given birth to her new lover's baby. Heer coldly explained how he wanted both his wife and her lover murdered and for their bodies never to be found. He offered the hitman £3,000, told him where to find his wife, provided her lover's car registration number and recommended the best time to kill him would be in front of his children as he collected them from school.

Unfortunately for Heer, the hired gun was me.

Heer, thirty-five, worked as an engineer for Land Rover in Coventry, and one of my best underworld contacts there tipped me off and introduced me to Heer at a hotel in the city, where every murderous word was captured on audio and video tape.

He arrived shortly after 6.30 p.m. in a battered Vauxhall Astra and I was introduced to him as the assassin who would carry out his dirty work. I was 'Neville', a disgraced soldier, cashiered for drug dealing, who knew how to use a gun and would pull the trigger on anyone, for a price.

Heer, a Sikh, was impressed and made it clear this was to be an 'honour killing'. His wife, who had also run off with his seven-year-old son, had brought shame on him. In the hotel room, he was calm and articulate and he smiled a lot. He explained:

> I don't know how this will work. Say they both disappear, killed, whatever you want to call it. They are gone.
>
> We do both of them. But it'll be no good if they get found.
>
> What we want is to just get rid of him [the lover]. I just want him out of my kid's life.
>
> I don't give a shit if he is deported or whatever, just get him out of the picture.
>
> Well, truthfully, the only way of getting rid of him is by killing the guy. Killing him. The body won't be found, will it?

Heer then moved onto the disposal of his wife. But his main concern was whether the police would link the killing to him. He said:

> Say they *both* disappear, killed, whatever you want to call

> it. They are gone. What is the comeback on me? I'm just
> scared of being caught, mate. That's all the bottom line is.
>
> The coppers will say straight away it's me. My family will
> be under investigation. What I'm worried about is, will any-
> thing come back if we get the missus out? Is that going to
> be too obvious?

Heer's eyes brightened at his own solution, suddenly realising the double killing would divert suspicion from him. He said: 'I could say to the coppers, "Officer, look, they have run away together." That would be more logical, wouldn't it? To outsiders looking in, they will say they have disgraced their families and legged it. It makes it look better.'

Relaxing on the hotel room sofa in a tracksuit top and training shoes, Heer revealed how much he hated the sight of his wife.

> I saw her yesterday and she had the baby on her shoulder.
> She tried to flaunt it in front of me.
>
> At the end of the day, in the eyes of the law, I can't do
> anything. I just get access to the son. And she has been the
> one messing around.

A brief flicker of mercy crossed his mind. 'I can't kill a child. The child is an innocent in all this.'

But he was quickly back to the business of murdering his wife, putting a price on her head and explaining he would have to borrow the money. 'I have to borrow money. The maximum I can borrow is £3,000. I'll approach this guy for the dosh. He will give me a cheque and that's it. Whatever you do, I don't want to know.'

Heer rose from the sofa, smiled and shook my hand. He was a slightly built, pleasant-looking young man. Inoffensive to the point of being non-descript. Well mannered and affable, even. But concealing a heart of total wickedness.

Soon after he left, I brought in West Midlands CID and handed them the tapes. Heer's feet didn't touch the ground. The police swooped and it would be several years before Heer would see the light of day again.

At the trial at Birmingham Crown Court, the jury heard that Heer's planned killing would have left his seven-year-old son motherless. They also heard how he had beaten his wife during their ten-year marriage.

The judge, Mr Justice Coulson, said:

> This was a detailed record of the key meeting you had with the hitman at the Hilton Hotel in Coventry. There can be no doubt at all what you were doing on that afternoon. The intended purpose, the murder of both your ex-wife and her lover. In my view, the transcript makes for chilling reading and only prison is appropriate.

He said there were a number of aggravating features, which included a clear statement of intent and Heer's lack of remorse and regret. Heer was sentenced to five and a half years in jail for soliciting me to murder Monica Heer and her lover Harsarup Mehmi.

Afterwards, Det. Sgt Paul Jones was kind enough to issue a statement. 'The *News of the World* investigation was of an exceptionally high professional standard and was impressive evidence in court. Undoubtedly, it was responsible for saving Mrs Heer's life and she will be eternally grateful.'

Det. Sgt Jones was meticulous, intelligent and patient but also worked from instinct. My favourite type of copper. But I am afraid he was wrong on two counts.

Mrs Heer was far from 'eternally grateful', sadly. I rang her to introduce myself after the trial and to wish her well. She mumbled something, said she had to go shopping and hung up. Thanks, Monica! Have a good life.

And I am afraid I must confess that my evidence-gathering was rather less than professional at one point. While waiting for Heer to arrive at my hotel room, I omitted to turn off the tape recorder in my pocket when I went to the lavatory.

In court, it is customary to play back all evidential tapes in their entirety, including even the 'Testing, testing, one, two three', in order to demonstrate the tape hasn't been cut or tampered with.

But on this occasion, the chief prosecutor felt it necessary to ask the judge if an exception could be made. The judge queried the request, noting it 'most irregular'.

'Perhaps, in the absence of the jury, we can play the relevant part to you in order to demonstrate,' the prosecutor gamely pleaded.

The tape recording sprang into life, amplifying through enormous speakers a thunderous noise like Niagara Falls, followed by the unmistakable sound of a trouser zip being hoist then the flushing of a lavatory cistern.

I could see the heaving shoulders of the assembled lawyers and detectives as I stood sheepishly in the witness stand. The judge's eyes widened, almost in astonishment at what seemed like the never-ending evacuation of the biggest bladder in Christendom. The ablution over, he dryly announced, 'Well, I see what you mean. I don't think much use will be served by its inclusion. In fact, it may even prove something of a distraction.'

Even in the midst of some of the darkest moments on the *News of the World*, I always found the comedy of the absurd was never very far away.

CHAPTER 21

THE MAX MOSLEY AFFAIR

IT'S IMPOSSIBLE TO pen this memoir without reference to the Max Mosley investigation and the subsequent legal fallout. It is also very tricky to write safely, as it has become a legal minefield. But it would be idiotic to ignore it. I will refrain from commenting on the legal judgment and whether we were right or wrong to publish it. The newspaper story has been read by countless millions of people all over the world. And you will all have your own opinion on the matter.

To navigate a course through this rocky terrain, I have decided to use the investigation's colourful and dramatic highlights as guiding beacons. These will not illuminate the full map, but they will hopefully provide you with a flickering torch to glimpse the inner workings of one of the most extraordinary newspaper stories in recent history.

It began with an anonymous call to the news desk in March 2008, which was then passed on to me. The male caller said he had very solid information that Max Mosley was organising a sadomasochistic orgy involving several prostitutes. He wanted to meet to discuss the matter.

It's almost impossible to believe now, but Max Mosley was an insignificant news figure at the time. He was president of the Fédération Internationale de l'Automobile (FIA), a non-profit association that represents the interests of motoring organisations and car users worldwide. To give him a grander newsworthy stature, one could add that the FIA is also the governing body for Formula 1. Still too dry to interest our readers. A Formula 1 racing driver, perhaps. But not an anonymous grey suit barely known outside the world of racing car rules and regulations. If it's still hard to believe his office came with such a barely noticeable public profile, his successor in October 2009 was Jean Todt, who has been in office almost five years at the time of writing. I imagine many of you are struggling to picture this person. That's how it was with Max Mosley in March 2008. Except with one remarkable fact, of course – Max Mosley was the son of the infamous Sir Oswald Mosley, leader of the British Union of Fascists in the 1930s and a figure reviled to this day. So when the anonymous caller revealed that Mosley Jr had ordered the prostitutes to dress as German soldiers, you may forgive my news antennae for twitching a little.

The assistant news editor who had passed me the tip, Neil McLeod, a decent newsman, hadn't even heard of Max Mosley and thought the whole thing a waste of time. I gathered together a selection of cuttings showing the history of his father, how young Max had helped him during his campaigns in the 1960s and that he represented 100 million members worldwide, many of whom would be aggrieved if their leader in anyway sexualised the plight of the victims of the Second World War. If it was true, we had a very strong news story and the strongest possible public interest defence, I argued. A meeting was arranged.

At the time I met Jason in the bar at Waterloo Station, I had no idea he was an MI5 officer, although I was later to guess, correctly, much to his shock and surprise. Our meeting was to have unforeseen and far-reaching consequences for many. And those consequences would reach to the director general of MI5 and Prime Minister Gordon Brown – and then to the High Court and to the courts in France.

But for now, as we sat in the bar, I listened as Jason outlined his tale. Short and with a boyish face, he seemed to be in his late thirties and he confided he had been a former Royal Marine, which accorded with his brusque efficiency and understated muscular physique. His partner, 'Michelle', was a professional 'high-class' dominatrix known as 'Mistress Abi', who provided themed orgies for Mosley at a basement flat on London's Embankment, he explained. And one such party was being scheduled for the coming week.

Throughout the course of the meeting and in subsequent phone calls, Jason claimed that a German military theme was being ordered and that he would have the details of where and when the orgy would take place.

I arranged a meeting with Jason and Michelle at their home in Milton Keynes. Michelle was a tall, 38-year-old blonde with a careworn face. She explained that in charge of the recruitment of the girls was 'Mistress Switch', another blonde from Milton Keynes, aged forty; that the orgy was to be the latest of many; and that it was to include German military uniforms, beatings, the mock rape of prisoners in striped uniforms, lice inspection, the barking of orders in German. It all had the flavour of a Nazi concentration camp to me and my colleagues at the *News of the World*.

I had several pieces of surveillance equipment with me to capture the evidence, and showed Michelle how to use it. Concealing surveillance equipment on a semi-naked girl who would inevitably discard much of her clothing in the process of an orgy proved tricky! In the end, I provided her with a tiny video camera to conceal in her brassiere and instructed her to stand several feet back from Mosley in order to capture any incriminating pictures, such as a Nazi salute.

On Friday 28 March, the orgy was set and I met Jason and Michelle off the train at Euston Station to go through final checks on the camera equipment in the back of my car and to finalise our contract with them. We agreed a fee of £25,000 for the publication of the story, and off they set.

Together with *News of the World* photographer Bradley Page, I waited outside Mosley's Embankment flat for the orgy's cast to appear one by one.

From 11.30 a.m. onwards, five prostitutes arrived in ones

and twos, all carrying bags with their uniforms and sexual paraphernalia. The first girl let herself in using her own key. Mosley arrived alone, smartly dressed and a suit, collar and tie and a navy mackintosh, looking nonchalant as he descended the stairs to the basement flat. It would later be revealed that he had been doing this for decades and such an event would have lost its feelings of trepidation and furtiveness long ago.

For a good hour, we waited in the car while the shenanigans played out inside. Then, one by one, they departed, with Michelle and 'Mistress Switch' leaving together to board the train back to Milton Keynes. I set off up the M1 to rendezvous with Michelle and Jason at their flat.

Giving complicated surveillance equipment to members of the public comes with a high degree of failure. In the panic of often stress-filled moments, the wrong buttons get pressed. Sometimes, they don't even get pressed at all. Wires become disconnected. Cameras get pointed at the ceiling, so you get a beautiful view of the cornicing and nothing else. Occasionally, the person simply 'bottles it', changes their mind and leaves the recording equipment at home. On such occasions as these, the reporter, not the member of the public, will be given a fierce dressing down by the news editor. If it was an especially big story, the dressing down could be fairly eye-watering. If it happened again, that would inevitably spell the end of big undercover work on the paper.

I was always lucky. Even when saddled with the biggest idiot in Christendom, they always managed to follow my simple instructions. And this day had been no exception. The quality of the video was A1. But the content was more extraordinary than we could ever have dared to imagine.

I cannot, for legal reasons, give you the detail and colour on this. Suffice to say, everyone at the *News of the World* office who saw it – the editor, Colin Myler; the barrister, Tom Crone; the deputy editor, Neil Wallis; the news editor, Ian Edmondson; the deputy news editor, James Weatherup; and the picture editor, Paul Ashton – all unanimously and instantly agreed it appeared to be nothing less than a Nazi-themed orgy. There wasn't even a debate about it.

A few days later, we published the now infamous splash, headlined 'F1 Boss Has Sick Nazi Orgy with 5 Hookers'. This was followed the week after with a second splash, an interview with Michelle, headlined 'My Nazi Orgy with F1 Boss'.

After the interview, while enjoying a drink in my hotel room with Michelle's husband Jason, I sensed he was hiding something from me. He had always refused to go into personal details about what he did for a living but this was nothing unusual among casual newspaper contacts. But there was something about his demeanour, his meticulous nature and his relaxed confidence that indicated he was more than just a former Royal Marine. His knowledge of international affairs was also extremely well developed for a soldier. I put it to him: 'You work for 5 [MI5], don't you?' He admitted it on the spot. It bonded us for a while. I shared my own involvement with his outfit, dropping the odd name, to reassure him.

It was also an extraordinary twist in the story. Jason was a surveillance officer, tasked with the responsibility of tailing major terrorist suspects. But his role was one we couldn't mention, unfortunately. He was our source and it was our duty to protect him.

However, it did lead to the most costly mistake in the whole investigation. Back at the office, the editor, Colin Myler, sensed the contact's new-found vulnerability and made a catastrophic error of judgement. Myler issued the instruction to haggle over the agreed £25,000 fee and cut it in half. I remonstrated with the news editor, Ian Edmondson, about it. Reneging on deals had become one of the hallmarks of the new regime and it had lost us countless contacts. I hated the practice, along with all the staff. But Edmondson and Myler pressed their case. He was only going to be a one-off contact, so there would be no long-term relationship to compromise.

It was grossly naïve. And naïveté is a dangerous flaw in journalism. The mistake was to lead to a catastrophic melt-down when Mosley decided to take legal action against us. Our one and only witness to the event was now embittered to us and the organisation surrounding us. I asked them to sign the revised contract and they reluctantly agreed. But we had lost their valuable loyalty.

This is an example of the creeping amateurism that began to pervade the *News of the World* in the years before its closure. When I first joined in the 1980s and for much of the next twenty years, the *News of the World* managed to outperform its rivals by deploying a very simple formula. As the most profitable Sunday newspaper on Fleet Street, we ensured that we not only paid the best on Fleet Street, but that we become famous for doing so. The most common phrase you would hear in the opening moments of a *News of the World* financial deal was, 'Don't worry, we'll look after you.' And by Jove, we did. Every member of the public knew it. This ensured an endless queue of people flocking to the *News of the World* with their story. We had so many, we had to be adept at diplomatically turning the grade B stories down. It was frequently admitted by staff on *The People* and the *Sunday Mirror* that every one of our page leads inside the paper would have been a worthy contender for their splash.

But all this began to whittle away with the new regime, which became known for taking delight in 'renegotiating' contracts at the eleventh hour. True, it could save money. But we became famous not for 'looking after' people but for giving the impression of ripping them off. By now, as chief reporter, I became a magnate for complaints from reporters who had become bitterly disillusioned. Valuable contacts were being 'burned' and were going elsewhere. And the weekend phones, which had once blazed off their hooks, providing the incoming Tuesday news desk with a plethora of stories, gradually began to fall silent.

So it was with this lazy approach that the *News of the World* entered the biggest privacy battle in the history of newspapers. The result was predictable. Michelle, our star witness, backed out at the last minute and failed to turn up at the High Court, where Mosley was suing us for damages. Stung by Myler and Edmondson's demand that she settle for half her promised fee, she felt betrayed and let down. Her response was to abandon us and go on Sky TV denouncing us and voicing bitter regret at having contacted us at all. Frankly, I cannot blame her.

Despite our genuinely held belief that Mosley had taken part in a Nazi-style orgy with a concentration camp theme, Mr Justice Eady ruled against us. I stood in the witness box and explained, in great detail, the manifold examples of role play that had led all of us at the paper to this conclusion. But we were unable to provide one single witness to actually explain what had been going on. Mr Justice Eady famously ruled in Mosley's favour and ordered us to pay a record-breaking £60,000 fine in damages. The legal costs ran to around £750,000. The German military uniform was Luftwaffe, not Nazi, and the lice inspections, striped uniforms, beatings and simulated rapes were meant to replicate a German prison and not a concentration camp. There were audible gasps in a packed public gallery when one of the women was heard on tape saying, 'but we are the Aryan race, the blondes'. This would clinch it for us, surely? No. Not part of a script, just a slip of the tongue.

At around the same time that Mosley's privacy case was fast-tracked to the High Court in a matter of weeks, Jason's role as a spy for MI5 rapidly unravelled. Mosley was keen to find out who was behind the sting and Jason was targeted by a surveillance team from Lord Stevens's investigation firm Quest. So, days after our article, when the MI5 man left his home in Milton Keynes, where he lived with his wife, he was followed by the detectives.

But the highly alert officer, well versed in anti-surveillance tactics, spotted the tail and rang his superiors. Fearing a major anti-terrorist operation had been compromised, MI5 went into a state of high alert and put its huge resources behind trying to identify the followers.

A team at MI5's headquarters at Thames House analysed his route home. Using traffic cameras and number plate recognition equipment, they soon established that he was being followed by a car belonging to Quest, a team of private investigators headed by Lord Stevens, former Met Police commissioner.

The Quest team apparently followed their target to Thames House. It was only then that they realised he was a security service officer.

High-level discussions between MI5 and Quest bosses then took place to ensure that no anti-terrorist operations had been put at risk.

Days later, Jason was forced to resign and the Mosley scandal led to a major review of MI5's vetting procedures.

This one article and the aftermath changed the newspaper landscape completely. It may be a cause of rejoicing for many that newspapers shy away from anything that looks like encroaching on someone's private life. But is has also ensured that those in power are no longer scrutinised with any degree of vigour.

But whatever my opinion in all of this, there are two indisputable legal facts: we lost, and Max Mosley won.

CHAPTER 22

THE CHRIS HUHNE AFFAIR AND THE ONE THAT GOT AWAY

ONE OF THE accidental hallmarks of my career on Fleet Street was the number of politicians I exposed for one misdemeanour or another. The list includes Robin Cook, Jeffrey Archer, Nigel Griffiths, Chris Huhne, Ron Davies, Nick Brown, Robert Hughes and several others – no wonder so many were gunning for me when they saw the *News of the World* suddenly crippled and on its knees!

The *News of the World* got these big stories not because I had an unbelievable array of contacts in the House of Commons (although I do have a few), but because I was often simply in the right place at the right time. Or because I managed to get there first. I was a well-connected reporter, but not *that* well connected. I always had very good sources in most of the government departments and within each main political party. But the most important factor in most of the stories I broke was luck. I was lucky. It is the same in business: whenever I've bought a house or a flat, the price has soared. The same with the first batch of shares I ever bought – they went through the roof. But I am neither a brilliant reporter nor a brilliant businessman. I'm just lucky.

My exposure of Chris Huhne, the then Climate Secretary, and his extramarital affair ended up having far-reaching consequences with both him and his wife serving jail sentences. How I came to break the story is a good example of the potent combination of being in the right place at the right time, being there first, having one decent contact and having a hefty dash of luck.

It began in March 2009. I received a call from a young chap who claimed to have some pictures of the married Labour MP Nigel Griffiths – one of Prime Minister Gordon Brown's closest friends – in a compromising position with a woman in his Commons office.

The pictures had been discovered by a work experience lad who had been seconded to Griffiths's office and they showed the MP with the woman dressed in her underwear and black stockings.

We were on fairly safe ground, as there was a strong public interest argument for running the story. Griffiths had carried out the tryst in his House of Commons office, thereby breaking the MPs' code of conduct. Worse still, he'd done it on Remembrance Day 2008. While the nation honoured its war dead, Griffiths had been using the seat of the legislature as a bedroom for his extramarital exploits.

I raced out to meet the lad. I say 'raced' because he'd also contacted our features department and they too were on their way. It had been a tactic of *News of the World* editors for fifty years to set the features and news departments at each other's throats. We dominated the Sunday market and, with no outside competition, internal competition was deemed to keep reporters on their toes. The editor Stafford Somerfield had introduced the inter-department rivalry when he took office in 1960 and it carried on until the paper closed.

So there was no chance of the editor calling features off. May the best man win.

On this day, my 'competitor' was my colleague Dan Evans. As I sped through London traffic, I rang the contact and warned him that a chap 'impersonating Dan Evans' was en route. And that he should avoid him at all costs as he was in fact an imposter working for the *Sunday Mirror* who would steal his story and expose him in the paper. He had to switch off his phone and meet me at a totally different location.

With Dan stranded and his line of communication cut off, I gathered the pictures and took them back to the office. The key to running the story was to prove the tryst took place in his House of Commons office. I memorised the scene and headed off to Westminster, where I was admitted by a contact. It's tricky getting access to an MP's office without an appointment. I lurked unseen outside for a few hours, hoping to get a glimpse when the door opened (I always fancied I was rather good at 'lurking unseen').

After a few hours, I needed to take the initiative before I was rumbled. I knocked on the door, Griffiths answered and I brushed him to one side and strode purposefully into his room.

'Are you the janitor?' I barked.

'Certainly not,' said the Prime Minister's best friend.

'Very sorry, wrong room then,' I replied as I turned 360 degrees and took in the scene. It was identical to the picture. Same ornaments, same litter bin, same sofa, same mock Gothic arch over the doorway. I'd seen enough to satisfy the News International lawyer and headed off, leaving Griffiths looking puzzled and a little flustered.

As I came through a corridor on my way out, a familiar face I hadn't seen in more than two decades beamed and came towards me, hand outstretched. After a quick catch-up, he finished with, 'Take a look at Chris Huhne. He's got a mistress. Don't know who but look hard enough and you'll find her.'

I suppose you're now all thinking, 'For goodness sake, why didn't you just start this piece by saying you were walking through the Commons when someone tipped you off about Huhne?!' Well, I thought I'd put it into context. Like so many of my stories, they all boiled down to simply being in the right place at the right time. And anyway, I like a good story!

Where to start with Huhne? He had a constituency home in Eastleigh, so I put a watch on that. After a week, one Friday night, a woman who was clearly not his wife arrived alone, lifted up a brick from the front door, took the key beneath it and let herself in.

A short time later, Huhne arrived and knocked on the door. The woman opened it and let him in. The pair stayed there the night. The following day, we watched as they attended various functions together. It was crucial to identify who she was. It might have been a relative, although their body language said not.

We decided to follow her to her London home and do an electoral roll check on who lived there. Following someone from Hampshire to London by car is not an easy feat and we lost her at traffic lights moments from her address.

Back to the drawing board. And back to the constituency address, where I was joined by my colleague Derek Webb, a former police officer with the elite South East Regional Crime Squad and the most gifted of surveillance experts.

A few weeks later, she was back. Same drill as the last time. But on the journey, we somehow managed keep on her tail unseen to base her at her London flat. The electoral roll showed her to be Carina Trimingham, a Lib Dem activist who was also on his Facebook site, as she'd helped him campaign on his failed leadership bid.

An internet search also showed she'd had a gay civil marriage, which had since ended.

The story was written. But the editor, Colin Myler, spiked it, judging Huhne was not famous enough.

Fast forward to May 2010. The election ushered in the coalition government and Huhne suddenly found himself Climate Secretary; if not at the very centre of government, certainly close to its heart. I lobbied hard to resurrect the story and Myler agreed we should look at it again.

Back to Eastleigh. And, like a lucky centre forward, five minutes later I saw Ms Trimingham arrive – quickly followed by Huhne. They stayed the night, leaving separately in the morning.

The following Sunday, the story ran on the front page of the *News of the World*. Huhne strolled into his Clapham home and told his wife Vicky that their 26-year marriage was over, then walked calmly off to the gym.

Distraught and confused and still in love with her husband, Vicky set about plotting her revenge and revealed how Huhne had previously arranged for her to take three speeding points on his behalf to escape a driving ban.

Isabel Oakeshott, the *Sunday Times* political editor, exposed the crime with a carefully crafted strategy of trust combined with clinical, journalistic efficiency.

But it's odd to think all this unravelling and domino effect would never have happened if a nosy teenager in 2009 hadn't picked up the phone to me. Or if I hadn't had the luck to bump into an old chum while lurking in the House of Commons!

However, while many exclusives came to me by chance, there were others that were hard fought for and yet never saw the light of day. Like hapless, boastful fishermen, reporters all have tales of 'the one that got away', and the one that stands firmest in my memory concerns a very senior politician indeed. One so famous, in fact, he would need no introduction to anyone in the Western world.

The tip came to me from a very reliable source in 2007 and it concerned a politician who had made much of his status as a family man. His slick PR team ensured photographs of him and his wife appeared frequently in the press. But all was not as it seemed, the tipster revealed. Instead, this politician had spent a considerable part of his life in homosexual affairs. The electorate was being duped, my source claimed, and the marriage was being used as part of a PR stunt.

Such a claim certainly merited investigation and I headed off to a remote part of central Spain. In a small rural village, one of the politician's former lovers was running a rustic but tasteful guest house with his gay partner, and I was told he would hold the key to the story. Unfortunately, the gentleman concerned wanted nothing to do with me and it looked like being a wasted journey.

The story was too good for the *News of the World* to give up on and for several days, I made various entreaties to him to talk. I called at the door, I rang the guest house and I sent letters, all to no avail. Part of the problem seemed to be his more dominant partner, who appeared to be doing everything he could to keep him from me. Every approach was being blocked by him.

I decided the only option would be to sit outside the café

about 100 yards down the street and watch and wait for him to leave the house alone.

Two days later (yes, life as a roving reporter certainly does have its boring moments!), out he came and, as he walked past the café, I invited him to have a coffee with me. After some delicate negotiations, over the next twenty-four hours he gave a full account of his story and of his relationship with the politician. The essence of his story was that, while working in London as a sales assistant in a men's outfitters in the early 1980s, he had been approached by the politician, who chatted to him and asked to meet him for a drink later in the week. A long, sexual relationship ensued, with the assignations taking place at the politician's London flat.

A crucial fact would have been the politician's precise address. But the source couldn't remember it. So I asked him to pin-point it on an A–Z. Using a map and describing the journey he took from the Tube station, I was able to pinpoint the address exactly. A check with the electoral register from the early 1980s revealed the name of the occupant: the politician in question.

This was extremely promising, because the address was not in the public domain anywhere easily accessible. He would have had to be on at least fairly intimate terms with the politician to pinpoint the address and describe the décor and furnishings.

This very reluctant witness gradually revealed his story, bit by bit. How the politician would leave early in the morning for work, leaving a note for his sleeping partner, and how it all fizzled out when the politician moved onto his next conquest. What shocked him most of all was how the politician had ended up getting married and flaunting his married status, especially during elections. The source was genuinely annoyed at the hypocrisy.

The following day, his partner found out he had been talking to me and contacted the politician through his website. The politician's reaction was furious. And he denied even knowing the man, let alone inviting him back to his flat.

This was especially telling as far as we were concerned. If he didn't know him, how did the man know precisely where he had lived all those years ago? How could he describe the furnishings – which I had managed to corroborate through a journalist who had visited at the time?

This ill-advised denial came perilously close to satisfying our lawyers that we were almost there with our story. But the private storm the politician had caused made our man retreat. Without him, there was no story. It was, as we say, 'spiked'.

If it hadn't been, the political landscape would have been radically altered.

CHAPTER 22

THE FUTURE OF THE TABLOID PRESS

CHAPTER 23

THE FUTURE OF THE TABLOID PRESS

PART OF THE point of writing this book was to show how most of our work at the *News of the World* was informed by old-fashioned journalistic techniques and not the various illegal newsgathering practices that have resulted in a whole raft of criminal trials. None of the events I have described involved voicemail intercepts or the payment of public officials; at least not to my knowledge.

However, it is important to stress that these illegal techniques have been rampant within our industry for years, if not decades. I was, to my regret, drawn into the conspiracy to intercept voicemails at the *News of the World*. I believed it to be in the public interest and so did our lawyers, who told me so. We were all dreadfully wrong. But ignorance of the law is no defence and we have been punished.

There has been a tendency to promote the myth that these techniques were confined within the walls of News

International (now News UK) – at the *News of the World* and *The Sun*. This, of course, is not the case and we are seeing journalists from several other newspapers now being arrested for the very offences which, lamentably, saw a big British newspaper close its doors. I hope we see no more. During my career on Fleet Street, journalists from many titles listened to voicemails or talked about having done so, *The Guardian* included. And before voicemails, in the 1980s and '90s, they would eavesdrop on actual phone conversations, especially in the pre-digital era. This is precisely how 'Squidgygate' was broken, when journalists listened to Princess Diana talking intimately to her close friend James Gilby in the late 1980s and the tape was published by *The Sun* in 1992.

We now also know that leading law firms and insurance companies have been using far more serious illegal techniques.

A report submitted to the Leveson Inquiry into press standards suggested hackers and private investigators were routinely paid to dig for information on companies and individuals.

Among the practices revealed by the confidential Serious Organised Crime Agency report, supplied to the Leveson Inquiry, were live telephone interceptions, computer hacking, police corruption and obtaining itemised phone bills.

I highlight this to show how illegal voicemail interception at the *News of the World* ought to be seen in the context of its prevalence within our own industry and others. When competitors were gaining an advantage by using these methods, and major, respected blue-chip companies were also breaking the rules, we followed suit. It doesn't excuse our behaviour but it perhaps helps explain it.

All of this does not make illegal newsgathering valid. Clearly, the press had got matters spectacularly wrong and it brought about the most cataclysmic storm in the history of newspapers.

There have been allegations of corrupt payments to public officials – soldiers and police officers – in return for stories. There have been gross invasions of privacy. And there has been phone hacking, a practice that has outraged a large section of the population.

So, what is the cure?

Ask a lawyer, and they will tell you: 'More law.'

Ask many politicians, and they will tell you: 'More state control.'

This is the default position of every lawyer and politician. More law. More political influence.

But law begets more law. Laws are seldom repealed, but tend to morph into Hydras, flaunting many heads.

And state control of the press, by whatever statutory instrument you may care to mention, is something I believe we should instinctively mistrust, as our ancestors have for 300 years.

Any form of state regulation of the press will have a stultifying effect on that most precious and hard-won privilege: freedom of speech.

The Leveson Inquiry has already had a damaging effect.

The recent conviction of Rolf Harris was jeopardised by his secret arrest, made possible by the Leveson Inquiry. In November 2012, police searched Harris's home and removed computer equipment and other items. He was interviewed under caution without being arrested. Newspapers merely reported that an unnamed television presenter in his eighties had been questioned.

Ironically, the questioning took place on the day the Leveson Report was published. One of its controversial suggestions was that except in exceptional circumstances, 'the names or identifying details of those who are arrested or suspected of a crime should not be released to the press or public'.

A few days later, Harris's lawyers, Harbottle & Lewis, sent a letter to at least one newspaper threatening dire consequences in the event of their client being identified, using the Leveson Report as their justification.

After Harris was arrested in March last year, Harbottle & Lewis despatched a threatening email to the *Mail on Sunday* containing similar threats, claiming that the public interest would not be served by naming him. The following month, Harris was finally identified by newspapers, and more than a dozen victims subsequently came forward, nine of whom testified at Harris's trial.

Justice was served, in part, by flouting Leveson, not by slavishly donning the shackles of his recommendations.

This position is backed by Keir Starmer, the former Director of Public Prosecutions, who said Harris's conviction may not have been possible if the sexual abuser had succeeded in keeping his name out of public view.

Even the merest hint of the threat of outside regulation and one Cabinet minister, the Culture Secretary Maria Miller, jumped on the bandwagon and was using it to crush a newspaper investigation into her expenses.

Miller's special advisor phoned the *Daily Telegraph* prior to publication in an attempt to warn it off. According to the paper, she issued a veiled threat by reminding it of Miller's role in enacting proposals in the Leveson Report on press regulation.

Even before external press regulation was properly debated, this politician couldn't resist using the threat of it to bury her misdeeds. She failed. And she resigned, shortly after the paper broadcast a taped call of her special advisor making the threat.

Recently, *The Spectator*'s assistant editor Isabel Hardman warned, grimly, that the number of politicians calling her office to demand they tone down their negative political stories has grown considerably since Leveson.

David Wooding, the *Sun on Sunday*'s political editor, says important political investigations are being, to use his very words, 'sanitised out of existence. Or simply spiked.'

And if the chill wind of censorship is being felt on the newsroom floor of *The Sun*, one of the most fearless publications in the world, just think how afraid the local press are feeling now. How daunting it is for them to probe the misdemeanours of their local council and individual officials and hold them to account, exposing wrongdoing to their electorate.

All this since the *threat* of outside regulation, not the implementation of it. With politicians using the threat of state regulation to beat the press into submission, just think what they would do if we gave them the lethal weapon of state regulation, forged in the law courts and finely honed on the ancient mastheads of our democratic free press.

For that is what it is. *Your* press. Not mine, a mere former custodian of part of it. And not theirs who seek to control it for their own political ends. *Your* press. It's an important mindset. The British press belongs to *you*. You cherish it because you know it speaks its mind. And in these days of slick, carefully stage-managed PR campaigns in business, politics and sport, it is a valuable free voice. A vital free voice.

Otto von Bismarck remarked, 'Politics is the art of the possible.' If political interference in the British press was made possible, it would be artfully and stealthily executed.

The misdemeanours at the *News of the World* and the investigations taking place into other newspapers have been used as an excuse by some to rush in a system that prevents papers from exposing scandalous behaviour by figures in the public eye. It is dressed up as a moral crusade about the right to privacy in the face of illegal actions by journalists. It is championed by celebrities such as Steve Coogan and Hugh Grant, who once courted publicity to boost their careers but seek to silence us when we expose their drug taking or their arrest for kerb-crawling.

Is it right that this cabal of disaffected celebrities and elitist quasi-academics should dictate what we should or should not read, like some latter-day Lord Chamberlain?

So what of that cure?

The cure is taking place as I write. The criminal wrong-doing by journalists has been investigated by 195 police officers for three years. As well as the trial which has just concluded, at least twelve more are in the pipeline, involving up to forty accused. They are among ninety-six journalists arrested since 2011. In July 2014, I was punished by an Old Bailey judge, alongside Andy Coulson, my former editor; Greg Miskiw, my boss; and my colleagues James Weatherup and Dan Evans for listening to voicemails.

I say this to demonstrate that the law works as it is. I can tell you from rather painful first-hand experience that wrongdoing is being severely punished. It is far more effective than moral puritanism. And it is far more effective than a Royal Charter, which may allow undue political interference and wipe out the industry with £1 million fines, or beat it into subservience with growing powers and influence in years to come, under less savoury political regimes than we enjoy at present.

We do not need a state cosh to beat the press. You have the police. You have the law. And you have the judiciary. It is enough. And I am the living proof.

EPILOGUE

POST
TENEBRAS LUX

AS THIS BOOK ends, a new dawn is beginning for me.

On 16 December 2014, I was appointed director of communications for the newly established Retail Ombudsman, helping to launch the scheme and acting as the interface between the organisation and the media, government and retailers. Like every great opportunity that is given to me in life, once again I can take little credit.

I've known David Hahn and his partner Julia for many years. They run a successful show-business agency in London called Celeb Agents. I dealt with David when I was on the *News of the World* and once did him a professional favour. It was a small gesture on my behalf but it meant a lot to David, an old-school show-business entrepreneur, for whom loyalty and straight dealing are ingrained in his gregarious and genial soul. He never forgot it. He introduced me to the consumer barrister Dean Dunham. After two meetings, I was hired to spearhead the media launch of the new Retail Ombudsman scheme.

To date, it has proved to be the most satisfying task of my career. My thanks to David, for continuously extending the hand of friendship. And to Dean, for entrusting me with a crucial role in his new organisation.

In an instant, my life shot in a completely new and exciting direction. In January, I formed Clear Vista Media and I've just opened a London office right next door to BBC Broadcasting House. It is a PR company. My role at the Retail Ombudsman is as a consultant, which has allowed me to take on additional clients, again from the Celeb Agents stable, including Jamie Allan, an astonishing Houdini-style illusionist who has regular gigs at the London Palladium and on TV, as well as a nationwide theatre tour. With Jamie and his deeply experienced manager, Joe Wenborne, I get to visit and wander around fascinating old Matcham theatres, watch audiences rise to their feet in delight and leave in a chattering buzz.

The *X Factor* winner Joe McElderry has also been a regular client, along with many others. As well as PR, it will be no surprise to learn I'm also doing crisis management advice. Having just survived reputational Armageddon after the News UK crisis, I help others to do the same.

One of the real perks of my job is that I always seem to get to hang around with fascinating people.

In the past few months, my work has taken me to the very heart of the media industry again. TV, radio and national, regional and trade press have all been incredibly generous in their willingness to engage with me once again, now the storm clouds have passed. I will be eternally thankful to them for that.

In my spare time, I've also set up TalentGB at TalentGB. com. It is a website for bands, musicians, singers, magicians – in fact, artists of every genre: rock bands, cover bands, jazz bands, ceilidh bands, big bands, crooners, Elvis impersonators, mind-readers, ukulele players, organists, comedians et al. Each one pays a modest £30 p.a. to upload their showreel, pictures and booking details, and we have more than 400 members. This has been incredible fun and a source of PR work too.

I also teamed up with one of my favourite broadcasters, James Whale, to work with him on *The James Whale Radio Show*, a cult podcast with brilliant ratings, often beating Graham Norton, Chris Evans and Jeremy Vine. TalentGB has supplied many of the bands that perform on the show, which can be heard from around forty outlets, including at TalentGB.com.

I first heard James as a teenager in the mid-1970s, when he was broadcasting for my local radio station, Metro Radio. He was acerbic, blunt, outspoken, opinionated and sometimes incredibly rude. I like people like that! But he is also incredibly original and that is a much sought-after commodity in broadcasting, which is why he has survived for so long.

So when he invited me on his LBC show around three years ago, I just couldn't say no. And we have been working together ever since.

With the extra time on my hands (although that has been in

rapidly diminishing supply), I have also found time to be the voluntary PR director for the charity Talking2Minds, which helps servicemen and -women suffering from post-traumatic stress disorder. It is run by a former SAS regular, Bob Paxman, a close friend of mine for many, many years.

There have also been numerous lectures, which I suspect will consume a lot of my time in the future, too. I've recently addressed the Oxford Union, the Cambridge Union and university and college students at Lancaster, Lincoln, Teeside, Kent, Wimbledon and my old school, Bede. It's incredibly rewarding and gives me the chance to give something back.

My main pillar of strength has been my wife, of whom you have heard so little. She soldiers on and breathes love and normality into our lives. And my daughters have provided me with what a dad in trouble needs more than anything else: their unwavering love and respect, which I could so easily have lost. For their love, I will be for ever grateful. Even through this crisis that has engulfed us over three and a half years, my young daughters soldiered on. Boo managed the highest grades in the entire country for two of her A level papers and went on to get a 2:1 in Classics from King's College London. And little Bee has just achieved five As, three Bs and a C in her GCSEs. I am now officially the thickest member of my household!

My mother, sister, brother-in-law, my 95-year-old father-in-law (a front-line veteran of the Battle of El Alamein in 1942) and my friends, many of whom I've known since schooldays, have all been bricks and I love them dearly for it. I will try to become increasingly worthier of their affection.

A special posthumous thanks to my mother's husband Bob Newton, who died in November 2014 and was loved by all of us. During the News International crisis, he told my mother: 'Don't worry. Whatever happens, Neville will always survive.' Those words were of enormous reassurance to my mother, who frequently repeated them back to me. He died just thirty-three days before his prediction came true.

So it's goodbye to all that. Farewell to Fleet Street. It was a crazy, hectic, exciting, dramatic, fascinating and ultimately dangerous time. And it was one heck of a lot of fun, for the most part.

But once again I find myself throwing all the pieces of the jigsaw of life into the air and watching where they all land.

My old school motto now seems to gather new meaning; Post Tenebras Lux – after darkness, light.

Time marches on. And so must I.

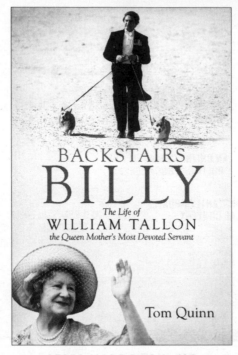